# Slammin' Skits

**Publisher:** David W. Welday III
**Editor:** Jim Kochenburger
**Associate Editor:** Christina Williams
**Editorial Assistant:** Cindy Carter
**Prepress Manager:** Jeanne Merola
**Prepress Coordinator:** Cathleen Kwas
**Production Coordinator:** Jenn Bouw
**Copy Editor:** Sandy Wright
**Interior Design:** Cathleen Kwas
**Cover Design:** Craig Davis and Kathy Stemley
**Cover Art Direction:** Jake Jones

### Contributing Writers:

| | | |
|---|---|---|
| Robert K. Arp | Todd Edwards | Mark Rempel |
| Gerard P. Bradley | Vicki Edwards | Jim Kochenburger |
| Cory Edwards | Mike Gillespie | Walt Weaver |

**CharismaLife**
PUBLISHERS

Copyright ©1997 CharismaLife Publishers
600 Rinehart Road, Lake Mary, FL 32746
Editorial Offices: (407) 333-7303
Toll-Free Order Line: (800) 451-4598
Library of Congress Number: 96-72173
ISBN 1-57405-183-0
First Printing: February 1997

All rights reserved. No part of this book may be reproduced in any manner whatsoever without written permission from the publisher. For information, write to the attention of the Copyrights/Permissions Assistant.

*Scripture taken from the HOLY BIBLE, NEW INTERNATIONAL VERSION. Copyright © 1973, 1978, 1985 International Bible Society. Used by permission of Zondervan Bible Publishers.*

# TABLE OF CONTENTS

What? Move the Pulpit?! ...................3

The Date ............................................6
    Topic: Embarrassment

Let the Witnessing Begin! ................11
    Topics: Witnessing, Sharing Christ

Who's for Lunch? ............................14
    Topics: Gossip, Standing Up for Other Christians

God's Love Never Gives Up
on Us ...............................................19
    Topic: God's Love

Oz Been Born Again! .......................23
    Topics: Salvation, Heart Changes

Contradictions .................................26
    Topics: Christian Love, Messages Our Lives Send

Lonely Larry Lebanowski ..................31
    Topic: Loneliness

One Christian Fits All .......................36
    Topics: Acceptance, Friendliness, Group Building

Jenny's Sin .......................................40
    Topics: Forgiveness, Response to a Christian Who Sins

Scripture in a Can ............................47
    Topics: The Bible, Power of the Word

Out From the Cold and Into
the Bold ...........................................51
    Topics: Boldness, Risk-Taking, Being a Doer of the Word

Defender or Pretender? ...................56
    Topics: Courage, Standing Up for What You Believe

Jacob Can Wait ................................60
    Topic: Sexual Purity

Benched ..........................................63
    Topic: Attitude

The Retreat ......................................69
    Topic: How to Process Spiritual Mountaintops

My Girlfriend's Back and There's
Gonna Be Trouble ...........................74
    Topics: Dating, Parents, Judgment

Mall Trip ..........................................79
    Topics: God's Favor, Prayer

Heart Beach ....................................83
    Topics: Righteousness, Holiness

Tested and Triumphant ....................88
    Topics: Trust in God, Victory

Darrell and Larry Discuss Jobs .........93
    Topics: Diligence, Self-Motivation

# WHAT? MOVE THE PULPIT?!
## By VickiJo Witty

When my husband and I started performing comedy in churches in 1975, we raised a few eyebrows. It just hadn't been done before. Although we were well received, people couldn't help noticing that preparing for a performance of Christian comedy was more trouble than preparing for a special speaker. On more than one occasion our need to set up on center stage sent us traveling long hallways and into the inner sanctums of boardrooms in order to gain permission to **move the pulpit.** (That was before the plexiglass ones had been invented, and churches usually had a holy half-ton mahogany edifice that hadn't been budged since Dedication Day 1949.)

Even using drama and comedy in your youth service calls for extra effort. But, after many, many years of setting up, tearing down, packing props, writing, rewriting, rehearsing, setting lights and checking sound, I want to assure you that the look of appreciation on the faces of your audience after you've brought the truth of God's Word to them in a powerful, fresh and creative way is precious, priceless and well worth the extra effort taken in "moving the pulpit."

## ARE YE FEARFUL?

Many youth leaders are apprehensive about trying drama and comedy sketches in their youth services. If you've ever stared into the silent eyes of 30 arm-folded teenagers after delivering what you had planned on being a hilarious punch line, then you understand why (and the true definition of "humiliation"). Besides this, it just seems like a lot of work (something most of us are not convinced we need more of). Performing drama and comedy to the "sight and sound" generation can be a scary thing if you have these or any number of hesitations. Here are some basics for doing drama and comedy that will help guide you into greatness.

## THE BASIC A, B, C AND D'S OF PERFORMING AND PRODUCING SKETCHES

### A Is for ACTING

OK, you don't have an auditorium full of trained thespians. Maybe you do have some people who would love to be in this week's sketch—maybe just one or two. Fantastic! Before you "compel" them onto the stage before their critical peers, challenge them to **ACT** by following these four "A" rules.

1. ANALYZE YOUR CHARACTER

   What kind of a family life does he (might he) have?

   What does this character probably feel about himself?

   With whom does he hang out?

   How does he walk, talk and stand?

   What kind of clothes does he wear?

   Encourage creativity, but remember that all information collected about a character should make sense when added to the facts already provided in the script. By filling in a character's background, actors personalize their characters. This process helps solve the ever-feared "flat, one-dimensional, robot syndrome" that strikes so many young actors.

2. ALWAYS STAY IN CHARACTER

   In order to move an audience, an actor must create believable emotion. In amateur settings there is a temptation to break character and giggle, yawn or (gasp!) wave at friends or family members. This temptation must be squashed. Tell your people to **stay in character** even when they're **not** delivering lines. Just because you're not talking doesn't mean you're not acting. Listen, nod, stand or do what that character would do.

3. ASSIGN YOURSELF TO THE PART

   Sometimes people are afraid to throw themselves into a part because they think they will look weird. Teach your actors that one sure way to come off weird is to hold back. Not giving your all to the part is the **very thing** that will make them look stupid. The more believable they are, the greater their impact, so encourage them to sell out!

4. **ABLE TO BE HEARD**

**Reality Check:** actors must **project**! Projection isn't screaming; it's talking loud, from the diaphragm. If you are not clear on this, ask a singer in your church to explain and demonstrate it to you and your kids. There are several exercises that can be taught to your troupe so they can **learn to be heard**. I often tell people, "How many times have you been told to be quiet or turn it down? Well, this is the place where you **can't** be **too** loud!" There are few things that frustrate an audience more than not being able to hear.

(*Note: If you are performing in a large auditorium, you should use microphones, but you must practice with them before the performance. Each actor should have his own mike and be trained in where to set the stand, how close to be, how to position it, how to turn the mike on and off and how to communicate with the sound person if there is a problem. Trust me, there are many things that can go wrong when combining young people and microphones, so* **rehearse with the mikes!***)*

## B Is for Blocking

Blocking is the designed movement of actors. That means planned entrances, exits, crossings, sitting, standing, reading, etc. It is the director's job (your job, unless you have enlisted another to be a willing "vessel") to read the script, to work out who moves where and when and then to make notes of that movement in her script. Later, in rehearsal, those notes are communicated to each actor during a "walk through."

WARNING: If this step is neglected, you run the risk of presenting a sketch that comes off confusing.

There are two basic laws in the World of Blocking around which all other rules spin:

1: Never turn your back on the audience.

2: Never draw attention away from where the audience's central focus should be. (This is termed "upstaging.")

Here are some "Do's and Don'ts" so you get the idea.

**DO:**

- Stay on the same plane with the person you are talking to. (If you stand upstage of another actor, you cause him to turn his back to the audience.)

- Make your crosses while **you** are talking. (If you move while someone else is talking, you draw the audience's attention and upstage the speaker.)

**DON'T:**

- Walk behind others while you are talking. (You upstage yourself by interfering with the audience's attention and view of you.)

- Point upstage with your "downstage arm." (It causes you to turn your back on the audience.)

**BLOCKING TERMS (AND HOW TO WRITE THEM IN SCRIPTS):**

| | |
|---|---|
| D | Downstage (forward; toward the audience) |
| U | Upstage (back; away from the audience) |
| C | Center stage (the approximate middle of the acting area) |
| L | Stage left (any area to the performer's left when facing the audience) |
| R | Stage right (any area to the performer's right when facing the audience) |
| X | Cross (stage) |
| ↓ | (can mean sit) |
| ↑ | (can mean rise) |
| | Variations should be self-evident. For example "UL" means upstage left of the acting area. |
| XC | Cross center (stage) |
| XDL | Cross down left (stage) |
| SDR | Cross down right (stage) |

## C Is for Cast

Tryouts are highly recommended. The director is responsible for choosing the cast, so he or she needs to set a time and place where people come and read out loud from the script. Then, the most talented **and** dependable people need to be given the parts. Can this be done without hurting anyone's feelings? Probably not, but rules and standards are good, remember? God uses them all the time. It is good to challenge young people to work and meet the high standard of the drama group.

## D Is for Director

What does a director do? Everything. The director usually chooses the script, the cast, the crew, the performance date and leads the rehearsals. She must be completely comfortable and familiar with the script so that when actors have questions, the director has the answer. Perhaps most important, the director sets the atmosphere in the cast. If a director takes a stern, demanding tone, the actors will follow. If the tone is upbeat and casual, the actors are more likely to experiment and be creative.

If you're planning to perform a sketch and you know that you only have one or two rehearsals before the performance, here's a checklist/rehearsal design to help you keep the basics covered.

**BEFORE REHEARSAL:**

____ Read the script **at least** four times.

____ Cast the roles.

____ Plan out the blocking and note it in your script.

____ Make out a prop and costume list and assign that responsibility to someone.

____ Know where you will rehearse and set up that area so it is ready.

____ If the script calls for special sound or lights, require the people who will be running those effects to be at rehearsal.

____ Make enough copies of the script so **all** players and technicians have their own copies.

____ Distribute the scripts.

## REHEARSAL: SEVEN STEPS TO A PERFORMANCE OF WHICH YOU CAN BE PROUD

1. **READ THROUGH**

    Open in prayer, then sit in a circle and read through the script from top to bottom three times. Don't waste time talking or take any time here to coach. Allow your actors to get familiar with the script and each other.

2. **WALK THROUGH**

    Give everyone a pencil, and starting with "lights up," walk through to "lights out," giving each actor his blocking directions. Again, don't try to coach acting here. This is for blocking only. Walk through it again to be sure everyone has his blocking. This is also the place for the director to make any needed changes in blocking. (If you have the luxury of one or two more rehearsals scheduled, this is a good place to stop and send them home with their scripts to learn lines.)

3. **EXPLORE**

    After explaining to the actors what you want from them, allow them to freely explore the scene now with their scripts in hand. Encourage them to get into their parts and experiment with their delivery. Make them use the blocking that has been given. (Got an actor who can't stand still? Have him do the scene once with his back constantly against the wall.)

4. **SET THE BUSINESS**

    "Business" is a stage word for small actions like drinking from a glass or using a handkerchief. Use the real props that are called for.

5. **COMB AND POLISH**

    This is the point where the director can stop, coach and correct every detail. Work with the actors. "Comb" through the lines then "polish" details of delivery and movement.

6. **WITHOUT STOPPING, WITHOUT SCRIPTS**

    Your goal is to perform the sketch twice straight through without stopping. Then you can go home.

7. **PERFORMANCE**

    Have your cast and crew arrive an hour before service. Everyone checks and sets his props; then do one more run through on stage to refresh everyone's mind. Reset everything again.

    Pray again and again for the skit, the actors, the rehearsals and performances. Give it all you've got and stand back in awe and wonder at the powerful impact drama can have in your ministry.

---

*VickiJo Witty is half of the Christian comedy team, "John & VickiJo Witty." They are widely known in Christian circles for their unique ability to communicate the gospel through comedy and drama. The Witty's reside with their three children in Tulsa, Oklahoma. They pastor Network Church and still perform in churches nationwide. For more information about John & VickiJo Witty call 918-274-7040 or write Witty Ministries, 11676 E. 21 Street, Tulsa, OK 74129.*

# THE DATE

## TOPIC: EMBARRASSMENT

**CHARACTERS**
Charlie
Cindy
Waiter
Pastor John

**PROPS**
Candle (or rose), small table, towel, two menus, two rolled napkins containing silverware, extra set of silverware, two glasses of water and tube of ointment.

*Set stage to look like a small, romantic restaurant. Waiter stands at stage right, waiting for the next guests to arrive and looking very serious about his job. He has a towel draped over his arm and two menus. The small table with a candle on it and two chairs are stage left. Charlie enters from stage right.*

**Charlie:** *[loudly to Waiter]* Hey! How's it goin', Jeeves?

**Waiter:** *[dryly]* Good evening, sir.

**Cindy:** *[enters behind Charlie and speaks sarcastically under her breath]* That's OK, I've got the door.

**Charlie:** *[oblivious]* Great! Well, let's grab us a few stools and gorge ourselves. Whaddya' say? *[Waiter starts walking them to their table.]*

**Cindy:** Charlie!

**Charlie:** What?

**Cindy:** *[whispering]* This is our first date, Charlie. Please don't be embarrassing.

**Charlie:** *[loudly]* Embarrassing? Honey, I'd have to belch the National Anthem in A minor to embarrass you in this place. Trust me.

# THE DATE

**Waiter:** Here is your table, sir. *[He pulls out the chair for Cindy and hands both of them their menus.]* May I start your evening with a refreshing beverage?

**Charlie:** Do you have free refills in a hoity-toity place like this?

**Waiter:** No, sir.

**Charlie:** We'll both have water. Do you charge anything for the lemon?

**Waiter:** *[not pleased]* No, sir.

**Charlie:** I'm just messing with you. Just two waters. *[Charlie picks up the rolled napkin by one end only, spilling the silverware onto the floor. He gets down on his hands and knees, trying to pick it up.]*

**Waiter:** Let me get that for you, sir. *[Waiter bends down as Charlie sits up. The two bump heads hard. Waiter pauses.]* Or not. *[Waiter walks away irritated and rubbing his head slowly.]*

**Charlie:** *[yells after Waiter]* I could sue you for that! And bring me some new silverware. *[Charlie sits down in his chair and tucks his napkin into his shirt collar]* See, I know how to treat the help in a place like this. Just do what I do. *[Cindy sighs.]*

**Waiter:** *[returns with two glasses of water and new silverware]* Have you decided what you'd like, or would you like to browse the menu a little longer?

**Cindy:** The poached salmon sounds simply delicious. Oh, Charlie, they have filet mignon!

**Charlie:** Filet McWhat? I don't want none of that sushi or nothin'! *[sees the prices for the first time]* My gosh! Have you seen the prices on this thing? *[looks at Waiter]* Are these prices in pesos or pennies?

**Waiter:** *[even more irritated]* I'll give you a little more time to decide. *[exits stage left]*

**Cindy:** *[whispers]* Charlie, please! If I had known you were like this, I wouldn't have suggested a restaurant like Lafayette's. *[aside, to herself]* I wouldn't have agreed to go out with you at all.

**Charlie:** What's that?

**Cindy:** Nothing.

# THE DATE

**Charlie:** *[suddenly scratches his right arm quite a bit]* Look at this, we can get appetizers as our meal and save a bundle.

**Cindy:** What's wrong with your arm?

**Charlie:** I've got this oozy rash that's been spreading. *[looks at his watch and pulls a tube of ointment out of his back pocket]* Actually, it's about time to put on my ointment. *[starts to undo the cap, then smiles and looks up at Cindy]* I know what will make you feel special on our first date—like we're a couple. *[Charlie hands her the tube.]*

**Cindy:** *[already looking disgusted but trying to stay polite]* Uh, no thank you. I feel special just knowing you considered me.

**Charlie:** You are a keeper! *[Charlie rubs some ointment on his arm, then wipes his hands on the tablecloth and puts the tube away while talking.]* Y'know, there's this orangutan exhibit at the zoo this month. You can actually watch their feeding, grooming, mating rituals and everything. Maybe we can go this weekend.

**Cindy:** *[gets very nervous and looks around]* Gosh, Charlie. I don't know. I think I have plans.

**Charlie:** *[takes off his shoes and stretches out his legs]* Maybe some other time.

**Cindy:** *[horrified]* What are you doing?! *[Waiter walks in, simply looks at Charlie's feet then walks back out.]*

**Charlie:** Just airing out my feet. These shoes are a size too small. *[reaches for his glass of water]* Is that OK? *[Knocks over the glass of water on the table and into his lap. Both Charlie and Cindy jump up from the table.]*

**Cindy:** I don't believe this.

**Charlie:** I know! These tables are so wobbly! This restaurant is going to pay for this! I'll be right back.

**Cindy:** *[sits back down]* I should leave while I can.

**Charlie:** *[walks over to stage right where Pastor John has just entered the restaurant]* Pastor John!

**Pastor John:** Oh hello, Charlie...long time no see.

# THE DATE

**Charlie:** Uh, yeah, well I've been awful busy with, um, school and...you know, school.

**Pastor John:** Man, I haven't seen you in youth service since last year, I think. Or was it the year before...

**Charlie:** So Pastor John, what's a youth pastor doing in an expensive place like this?

**Pastor John:** Oh, I'm meeting Pastor Dickens here for dinner. *[notices Charlie's soaked clothing]* What happened to you?

**Charlie:** I'm on my first date with this girl Cindy and the tables are really wobbly...well, it's a long story.

**Pastor John:** First date, huh? What's she like?

**Charlie:** She's a little weird, but I think I could get used to her.

**Pastor John:** She's weird, is she? What church does she go to?

**Charlie:** Uh, I don't know.

**Pastor John:** *[looks past Charlie to Cindy sitting alone at the table]* She looks like a very nice girl, Charlie. Is she a Christian?

**Charlie:** Yeah. No. I don't really know. She looks like one. The subject never came up.

**Pastor John:** Charlie, that's a very important part of a relationship. It all starts on the first date. *[pause]* Why didn't you feel you could talk with her about your faith?

**Charlie:** *[uncomfortable and bashful]* Aw, c'mon Pastor John, just bring up a sticky subject like that out of the blue? That's something I couldn't do! That would have to be the number one, most embarrassing thing in the whole world! See ya, gotta go.

*[Charlie leaves as Pastor John nods his head slowly in an incredulous "Oh, I see..." manner]*

# THE DATE

## DISCUSSION

1. Why was Cindy embarrassed? Had you been in Cindy's place, how would you have reacted? What would you have done? Why?

2. Tell us about your most recent embarrassing experience and how you responded to it. Why did you respond as you did? How would you like to have reacted differently?

3. How do you typically respond to embarrassment? Select all that apply. *(Consider writing responses to this question on a chalkboard if you have one.)* Why do you respond this way?
   a) become angry
   b) try to embarrass someone else
   c) laugh it off good-naturedly
   d) stay quiet and don't react outwardly, just feel bad about myself
   d) all the above
   e) other _____

4. Read or summarize Esther 3; 5:9-14; 6:1-12; 7:1-10. Much can be learned from looking closely at Haman's reckless and angry handling of his embarrassment. What incident involving Mordecai proved to be quite embarrassing to Haman? Why? How did he choose to react to his embarrassment? How did his anger and desire to retaliate by humiliating Mordecai only make matters worse? How did the story finally end?

5. What can we learn about handling embarrassment from Haman's mishandling of his embarrassment?

6. What advice would you give to a friend who is embarrassed about something he or she did and is taking it hard?

7. Knowing what you know now, how many of you would react differently to the embarrassing experience you named earlier? How?

8. What one thing can you keep in mind to keep from tearing yourself down when you suffer embarrassment in the future?

# LET THE WITNESSING BEGIN!

## TOPICS: WITNESSING, SHARING CHRIST

### CHARACTERS
Barry (dressed overzealously in Christian T-shirt, Christian bumper stickers, pins, etc.)
Linda
Guy

### PROPS
Table, comb, yo-yo, Frisbee with "Jesus" written on it, bundle of pencils, backpack, huge Bible and elements of Barry's attire.

*Barry sits next to Guy at study table as if in school library. Guy seems to be at wit's end and has begun gathering his books.*

**Barry:** So the chemical reactions you're studying here are **nothing** compared to the way Jesus reacts with your life! The equation is simple! E-ternity equals J.C. squared!

*[Guy leaves, shaking his head. Barry calls after Guy.]* The molecules of salvation can bond with yours! Make God your nucleus! Pray with me!

*[addresses audience, proudly]* Witnessing? Yes, I am! Another lost soul got away. *[yells after Guy]* But I'll getcha next time, buddy! *[addresses audience]* I'm not just tellin' em. I'm screamin' it from the mountaintops! I'm a fireball for Jesus! I come fully equipped! Someone needs a pencil? Boom! *[whips huge bundle of pencils out of his backpack]* I've got John 3:16 printed on each one!

Here's a sly one. *[pulls out a comb]* I approach a heathen with tangled hair. "Excuse me, but I couldn't help noticing that you need to comb your hair." As he begins to groom himself, I say, "You may notice that there's a message written on the comb"—and the witnessing begins! Just like this Jesus Frisbee! *[pulls out Frisbee]* Guide me, oh Lord! *[He flings it out randomly over group members and a loud thump is heard.]*

**Guy:** *[offstage, yells]* Ouch! Hey!

# LET THE WITNESSING BEGIN!

**Barry:** Be blessed, my friend. Ye have been pegged in the head that ye may be saved!
*[From offstage Guy throws Frisbee back at Barry. Barry ducks.]*

Some people don't want to listen to me. A lot of them just run the other way when they see me coming. That's cause they feel the fires of hell licking at their ankles!

*[Linda enters as Barry sits back down.]*

**Linda:** Barry, as a fellow Christian, I've been meaning to talk to you about...ummm... your approach.

**Barry:** Just getting the ball rolling, Linda. Look, this is my favorite. *[produces a yo-yo]* You see, it's an "I-Love-Jesus" yo-yo. It says it all so clearly...Jesus died...*[lets yo-yo spin at the bottom of the string]*...and rose again! *[snaps it back up]* Do you feel the anointing? They play with the yo-yo, and then the witnessing begins!

**Linda:** No! No, it doesn't. Nobody wants to read your T-shirts or hear your stupid metaphors anymore.

**Barry:** Because they're deep in sin?

**Linda:** No, because you irritate them.

**Barry:** But...

**Linda:** *[holds up hand as if to say "hear me out"]* Look, this is not some Jesus Fan Club you're recruiting for. You're supposed to listen to people, too. Be a real person with them. Love them. Be a friend first, and when the time is right, God will make you sensitive to say and do the right things.

**Barry:** *[offended, but also trying to understand]* So you're telling me I put Bible story toilet paper in the bathrooms for nothing?

*[Linda puts her hand to her forehead and shakes her head.]*

**Linda:** I don't want to think about that right now. The point is that...

**Barry:** The point is that you want me to do what most other Christians do—sit idly by while most of the people they know go to hell.

# LET THE WITNESSING BEGIN!

**Linda:** Barry, you're missing my point, I'm just saying that witnessing is first and foremost about loving people and...

**Barry:** *[distracted by someone he sees approaching]* Linda, I appreciate you sharing this with me from your heart. I really am going to think this over, but first *[gets up]*...gotta go! I see the wrestling captain, and I've got a good word for him! *[leaves while calling out dramatically]* Rick! There's a wrestling match going on in your soul! I'm here to pin you with Jesus!

*[Linda sits and shakes her head sadly.]*

## DISCUSSION

1. What is Barry's strength in witnessing? What is his biggest weakness? Why?

2. How are you most like Barry? most unlike him? Why?

3. Read one or more of the following passages: Philemon 1:6; 2 Corinthians 3:1-3; Matthew 5:13-16 and Acts 17:16-34. What do these passages say about how to witness? What do they say about the kind of witnesses we should be? According to Philemon 1:6, what benefit will we ourselves gain from being active in sharing our faith? Explain how you believe this works.

4. What is the best way you have found to witness (share Christ) to another person? Why? Which was most effective for reaching you when you did not know Christ? Why?

5. When was the last time you thought about witnessing to someone or felt God was telling you to do so? What did you end up doing? Why?

6. What has God done for you? How might this be a blessing or encouragement to someone who does not know Jesus personally if you told him about it?

7. What one thing will you do to become more of a bold witness for Christ? Why?

# WHO'S FOR LUNCH?

## TOPICS: GOSSIP, STANDING UP FOR OTHER CHRISTIANS

**CHARACTERS**
Ramona
Todd
Andrea

**PROPS**
Lunch trays, real (or fake) food, compact and lipstick.

*Ramona and Andrea are in the school cafeteria eating.*

**Ramona:** *[looks dreamy]* Anyway, all I can do is think about Todd; he is sooo good-looking. And, you know, I feel different this time. I mean, Todd and I, what we have—it's mature. I think this one is true love.

**Andrea:** *[looks nauseated]* That's...um...great! Does Todd know about your mature relationship?

**Ramona:** Ha, ha! Some things you don't have to spell out; it's a word, a glance, a smile, an innocent hello in the halls, and something mysterious and magical happens. Time stands still...an unspoken connection is made...and you both just know, you know?

**Andrea:** *[sarcastically]* No. So he has no idea you like him?

**Ramona:** Honestly, Andrea, you are so immature. I didn't think you would understand these deep matters of the heart. Why do I even hang around a romantically-challenged person like yourself?

**Andrea:** Pardon me, Miss "Called-Me-on-the-Phone-Before-I-Went-on-My-Date-Last-Friday-Night-to-Cry-Because-*[whiny voice]*-I-Don't-Have-a-Date."

**Ramona:** *[pouts]* That was way harsh, Andrea.

**Andrea:** Oh, I'm sorry; I was out of line. Friends again?

# WHO'S FOR LUNCH?

**Ramona:** Friends again! *[They quickly hug, then look around self-consciously.]*

**Andrea:** Back to the Todd channel. *[pauses]* I don't know quite how to put this but...look, you're no saint, and I hear Todd's one of those born-again Christian types. You know, the kind who talks to God and He *[eerily]* talks back!

**Ramona:** *[mischievously]* Well, we'll just see how Christian he is when I turn on my famous womanly charms. *[puts on lipstick and looks at herself in her compact mirror]*

**Andrea:** *[suddenly alert]* Don't look now, Miss Womanly Charm, but here he comes. Todd alert! Todd alert! *[siren noise]* Whee-oh-whee-oh.

**Ramona:** Ohmigosh, oh no! Is anything hanging from my nose? Is anything sticking in my teeth? Is he looking?

**Andrea:** He's coming closer. Yes, you do have something in your nose, and something green is sticking in your teeth. *[Ramona frantically rubs at her nose, primps and picks furiously at her teeth]* But it's OK, he's going the other way now. *[Ramona collapses in relief]*

**Ramona:** Oh, thank God! If Todd knew how much I loved him, I would just die! *[Todd walks up right behind her as she says this.]*

**Todd:** Excuse me, is anyone sitting here?

*[Ramona shoots Andrea a nasty look. Andrea snickers.]*

**Ramona:** *[whispers to Andrea]* I'm going to kill myself, but first I'm going to kill you! *[brightly to Todd as she tosses her hair]* Oh, no one's sitting here; you're welcome to it!

**Todd:** Thanks.

*[Girls don't know where to start.]*

**Andrea:** So...how's God doing these days?

*[At first Ramona nods her head in agreement, but then she looks at Andrea with shock.]*

# WHO'S FOR LUNCH?

**Todd:** [*not sure how to respond.*] Ummm...He's doing fine—a little disappointed with yesterday's sunset, so He has something special planned for today. [*Andrea nods her head enthusiastically, then figures out Todd is kidding her when Ramona pokes her in the ribs.*] He told me to tell you He wants to speak with you.

**Andrea:** [*alarmed*] He does? Wait, you're kidding me again, right?

**Todd:** Sure I am. But it's true, He would love to talk to you. [*He looks down at his food. Andrea makes "he's crazy" gestures and points to Todd.*]

**Andrea:** Just tell Him to page me.

**Todd:** [*smiles*] No problem.

**Ramona:** [*desperate to change the subject*] So, Todd, did you hear about the stupid thing that Tammy Miss "Homely-Uglier-Than-a-Toad" did yesterday?

**Andrea:** Oh, that! She isn't just ugly; she is soooo stupid!

**Todd:** You mean Tammy Centel who goes to my youth group? Uh, no, what happened to her? [*Ramona and Andrea pause to make "ouch" expressions, but continue.*]

**Ramona:** Uh, yeah. It happened in math class. Everyone knows you don't ever ask questions in Mr. Clark's class. It's suicide.

**Todd:** What did she do?

**Andrea:** We were going over some pre-algebra stuff. Nobody understood it, but at least we knew to shut up about it. Tammy asked Mr. Clark to explain this problem he was solving on the board. She didn't get it.

**Ramona:** He went ballistic with her and made her come up to the front of the room and do the problem herself. We were all sitting there laughing because she is soooo stupid.

**Todd:** I don't think that's very funny. I hope she's OK. We've prayed a lot for her at group about that class.

**Andrea:** Prayed...for her...for a class? Ohhhh. Come on, Todd. You know how geeky Tammy is. Everyone makes fun of her. I've even heard people from your youth group say stuff.

# WHO'S FOR LUNCH?

**Ramona:** Tammy does have...nice hair. *[Andrea and Todd both give Ramona a puzzled look.]* It's got those cute little swirly things.

**Todd:** Look, I'm not sure any of us are so together that we can be judging Tammy. Right now I'm feeling bad for her.

**Andrea:** Oh, come **on**! Nobody could care about Tammy Centel—it's a sociological impossibility. Quit the goody-goody act.

**Ramona:** I agree...I mean, with Todd. I'm feeling kind of bad myself right now. *[gives Andrea dirty look]* So what about this lunch, could it get any worse?

*[Andrea and Todd again both give Ramona a puzzled look.]*

**Todd:** Andrea, this is no act. God is real to me. I live my life to please Him, in every way. That means I don't gossip. It means I stand up for my friends. You can know Him like I do.

**Andrea:** God talk, God talk! *[Andrea holds her hands over her ears and squeezes her eyes shut. An awkward silence follows.]*

**Todd:** Well...I've got to be going. Later! *[Todd gets up and leaves the table.]*

**Ramona:** *[panicked]* B-b-but Todd...wait....um...wait...we're sorry! *[drops head to table]*

**Andrea:** *[nervous, trying to recover]* Get that, will you? Mr. Goody-Goody Perfect Christian just put us down. No big deal! Who needs him?

**Ramona:** *[head shoots up]* Now I am going to kill you! *[Ramona chases Andrea out of the cafeteria.]*

# WHO'S FOR LUNCH?

## DISCUSSION

1. What was happening here? How well do you feel Todd handled this situation? Why? Could he have handled it even better? How?

2. Tell us your most recent, worst experience with gossip (either as the gossiper or the one being gossiped about). Or, tell us of your worst experience of being betrayed by a friend who did not stick up for you when you needed him.

3. Although Tammy didn't hear what Ramona and Andrea said about her, both girls seemed a little ashamed of their words when Todd said he knew Tammy and refused to join in their gossip. Why? Have you ever stood up for someone or stood against gossip as Todd did?

4. Read one or more of the following passages: Proverbs 16:28; 18:7-8; 26:20; Galatians 5:13-16; 6:2,9. What is the final outcome of gossip? If someone gossips, what does this say of his or her character? How have you been hurt in the past by gossip? by a fellow Christian not standing up for you? How has this changed you or affected you in the way you treat others? Why?

5. Cite some possible scenarios where someone might be most tempted to gossip or to not stand up for another Christian. For example, a friend walks up to you and says that a certain enemy of yours is gossiping about you. Your friend has some juicy gossip of her own she would like to share with you about your enemy, etc. *(Write these on a chalkboard or discuss them each as they are suggested by group members. Brainstorm with group members ways to respond that avoid gossip and harming people with words. Also discuss why it is important for Christians to stand up for one another against opposition.)*

6. What will you keep in mind the next time you are tempted to gossip or to not stand up for a Christian brother or sister? What will you **do** the next time you are tempted to gossip about someone? tempted not to stand up for another Christian?

# GOD'S LOVE NEVER GIVES UP ON US

## TOPIC: GOD'S LOVE

## CHARACTERS

Mark Winkendollar (cheesy and swanky game show host who smiles constantly and frequently points at the audience while trying to look groovy)

Betty (contestant)

Voices of:
  Mr. Peterman
  Mrs. Leiberwitz
  Sandra
  God

## PROPS

Two microphones, pulpit (or music stand), photos, cassette of cheesy game show music and cassette player.

*Pulpit and contestant's microphone sit center stage for contestant. Play music as Mark runs out on stage with a microphone in one hand.*

**Mark Winkendollar:** Hey, Hey! Welcome to the jazziest show in the biz—"Guess Who Has Given Up Now!" I, of course, am your host of all hosts, Mark Winkendollar. *[Waits for audience to applaud. If they do not, he eggs them on until he gets a response he is pleased with.]* Let's welcome our contestant today. She is a lovely darling from the Northwest. Let's welcome Betty!

**Betty:** *[runs out on stage, jumping up and down]* Oh my gosh, oh my gosh! I can't believe I'm finally here! I love you, Mr. Winkendollar! I love you!

**Mark Winkendollar:** Whoa, Betty. Watch the suit. OK, let's snap on over to the coolio cool contestant's stand and get this funky game going. *[Mark leads Betty over to the contestant's stand.]*

**Betty:** *[leans to talk into Mark's microphone]* I'm so excited!

**Mark Winkendollar:** *[annoyed, points to Betty's microphone]* Here, Betty, this one is just for you.

# GOD'S LOVE NEVER GIVES UP ON US

**Betty:** *[almost out of breath from excitement]* Thank you. Thank you so much.

**Mark Winkendollar:** *[looks at Betty as if she's a freak, then turns to the audience with a cheesy smile—back to his normal self again]* Now, I know everyone here today knows the fabulous rules of this crazy game. We will all prick up our ears to listen to the zany voices of people in Betty's life, and dear, sweet Betty will try to—say it with me— *[extremely dramatic]* "Guess Who Has Given Up Now!" Let's begin with this one.

**Mr. Peterman:** *[voice only from offstage]* Betty, I thought you showed real promise. You usually could hit the ball, and although you wore funny shoes, your uniform was always neatly pressed. But you're pretty excitable and don't come to practice on time. You're a sweet girl, Betty, but I don't think you're focused enough for the team.

**Mark Winkendollar:** That's clue number one, Betty. Do you have any idea who it could be?

**Betty:** *[concentrates hard for five to ten seconds, then answers slowly]* I guess that *[pauses]* Mr. Peterman, my volleyball coach, has given up on me now. *[looks expectantly at Mark to see if she's right]*

**Mark Winkendollar:** Audience? Do you think our sweet Betty is right? *[looks at Betty]* You **are** right, Betty! Congratulations! One down and just three to go. Are you ready?

**Betty:** *[so happy she looks as if she is going to cry or faint]* I can't believe it. I'm so excited.

**Mark Winkendollar:** Really? You're excited? Moving on...in our fun, groovy half hour of weekday mischief, we have a second voice for you today, Betty. Can you guess who it is?

**Mrs. Leiberwitz:** *[voice only from offstage]* You are the most pathetic student I have ever had. You never practice. You must be tone deaf, and you look funny. I gave up on you the second you walked in my door.

**Mark Winkendollar:** Well, Betty...

**Betty:** *[without hesitation and very excited]* I guess that Mrs. Leiberwitz, my piano teacher, has given up on me now!

**Mark Winkendollar:** That was obviously an easy one for you, but wait until you hear this.

# GOD'S LOVE NEVER GIVES UP ON US

**Sandra:** *[voice only from offstage]* I'm sorry, Betty. I thought I could share anything with you, but you told Brad Lloyd that I thought he was hot. Now I can't even be in the same room with him. You embarrassed me.

**Mark Winkendollar:** Wow! What a confession. No wonder the girl is giving up on you, Betty! After this first clue, do you know who it is?

**Betty:** *[thinks hard for five to ten seconds]* Well, it could be...no that was John Hull...it might be Tammy...no, that was a different secret. *[gives up reluctantly]* I'm afraid I need a second clue, Mr. Winkendollar.

**Mark Winkendollar:** Oh, Betty, that'll cost you a snazzy point or two, but here's the second clue.

**Sandra:** You've run over my cat with your Volkswagen bug—twice. You always eat all of my chocolate and then leave sticky candy wrappers in my locker. You have horrible breath. I can't be your best friend anymore.

**Betty:** *[excited once again and answers without hesitation]* I guess my best friend, Sandra, is giving up on me now! *[Betty jumps up and down clapping, knowing she got is right.]*

**Mark Winkendollar:** You do know these are actual testimonies, don't you, dear Betty? *[Betty looks sad with realization, but Mark cuts into her moment with his game show drivel.]* Way to go, Betty! You have conquered three out of four rounds. You are on your way to victory! *[Betty smiles and is excited once again.]* Now, pay close attention! We have arrived at our bonus question, and this one's tricky. Are you listening closely? *[Betty nods.]* Betty, see if you can guess who this is.

**God:** *[voice only from offstage]* Betty, I will never give up on you. I don't care what you've done, what you're doing right now or what you'll do in the future. I will always be here for you. You are My first priority, Betty, and you can always count on My love for you.

**Betty:** *[jumps up and down]* My dog, Sparky! It's my dog, Sparky! I'm so excited! I'm so excited!

**Mark Winkendollar:** Ooooh, Betty. I'm sorry. The correct answer is God. *[There is brief silence while the realization that she just lost the game sinks into Betty.]*

**Betty:** I was wrong?

Page 21

# GOD'S LOVE NEVER GIVES UP ON US

**Mark Winkendollar:** I'm afraid so, Betty. God is the correct answer. The "Almighty Creator of the universe, the only One in the history of history who will never ever, not in a million years, not even when you die, give up on you" kind of God.

**Betty:** I was sure it was Sparky.

**Mark Winkendollar:** Nope. As a matter of fact, I have photos here showing Sparky taking the trip to Maui that you would have enjoyed had you won. He looks great with a tan, don't you think? *[Betty starts to cry.]* Hey, to all you homo sapiens out there in TV land, join us next time for—say it with me—"Guess Who Has Given Up Now!" Bye-bye.

## DISCUSSION

1. If you had been Betty, would you have recognized the words as God's? Why do you think Betty didn't?

2. When have you doubted God's love for you? What caused you to doubt His love? Why?

3. Is it typically easy or difficult for you to believe God loves you? Why?

4. Read Isaiah 54:9-10. Say this passage in your own words. What does God promise in verse 10? When have you most strongly felt God's love? Why? Read 1 John 4:7-12. When have you seen someone most powerfully express God's love to another person? How important is it for us to love others? Why?

5. If a non-Christian friend of yours asked you what proof you had that God loves you, what would you tell her? How do we experience God's love?

6. What one thing will you do today to remind yourself of God's unconditional, never-ending love for you? In what one way will you express God's love to someone else?

# OZ BEEN BORN AGAIN!

## TOPICS: SALVATION, HEART CHANGES

### CHARACTERS
Dorothy  
Tin Man  
Scarecrow  
Lion  
(all costumed as closely as possible like the characters in the Wizard of Oz)

Giz (dressed like a generic used car salesman)

### PROPS
Thick-rimmed glasses, briefcase, cardboard heart on a yarn necklace, sunglasses, two small balloons and cardboard cupid bow, arrow and wings.

*Dorothy, Tin Man, Scarecrow and Lion are skipping and singing "Follow the Yellow Brick Road." Giz enters.*

**Everyone:** Are you the Wizard of Oz?
*[except Giz]*

**Giz:** Not exactly. It seems that the Wiz is somewhere in Little Rock visiting family. But do not fear, I will be able to take care of any request you might have.

**Dorothy:** W-W-Well...who exactly are you?

**Giz:** I'm the Gizzard of Oz! It's sort of like a green belt in karate. First you're a blizzard, next a gizzard, then a lizard and ultimately the grand poobah, the big daddy, the head honcho of them all—the Wizard of Oz! I shall grant any request that you might have, without any cost or limitation. However, tipping is permitted...uh...hmm. Yes. *[arches eyebrows hopefully]*

**Scarecrow:** Duh-ahhhhh-Yuh...Mr. Gizzard, I am so glad we found you. More than anything else in the world, duhhhh, I want to have a, duhhh...a brain! Yeah...dat's it!

Page 23

# OZ BEEN BORN AGAIN!

| | |
|---|---|
| Giz: | *[sarcastically]* All you want is a brain? Intelligence is far over-rated. Multi-media brain deadness is IN. Wouldn't you much rather have just have a few days alone in the house to watch mind-numbing music videos?...a day of mindless thrills at an amusement park? OK, OK...a week being mauled at the mall? |
| Scarecrow: | Nope...I wanna get some a dem brains. |
| Giz: | OK, kid, let me tell you what I'm gonna do. *[pulls out glasses and briefcase]* All you need are a few external changes. Here, put on these glasses and carry this briefcase. Now, don't you look smart! |
| Scarecrow: | Duh-ahhhh...Mr. Gizzard, me don't feel no smarter, duhhh. *[mouth is open, gaping]* |
| Giz: | You aren't, but don't let that bother you. Image is everything. Right, kid? |
| | *[Giz grabs head of Scarecrow, moves it up and down and closes his gaping mouth. Scarecrow smiles.]* |
| Tin Man: | Gosh, that was great, Mr. Gizzard. Perhaps you can help me. You see, more than anything else in all the world, I want a new heart. |
| Giz: | You know, kid, what you want and what you need are two totally different things. Let me tell you what you need. You don't need a new heart. *[pulls out cardboard heart on yarn necklace and hangs it around Tin Man's neck]* You just need this! There, that ought to fool everyone. Just in case, though, you will need to wear this. *[pulls out cardboard cupid bow, arrow and wings]* Now, don't you look like you have a heart? |
| Tin Man: | I don't feel like I have a new heart. I just feel stupid. |
| Giz: | Stupid...Cupid...what's the difference? |
| Lion: | P-P-Please help me, Mr. G-G-Gizzard. I-I need a n-n-nature that's p-p-powerful. |
| Giz: | *[whispers]* Come on over here. I think I can help. *[When Lion relaxes, Giz shouts "Boo!" and snorts out a laugh as Lion jumps.]* Hey, kid, you don't need a new nature filled with power and boldness, what you need is the Schwartzenegger special. *[pulls out sunglasses and two small balloons]* These glasses will cover up your fear, and make sure you put these balloons in your sleeves. *[Lion does this.]* That's better. Now always remember to say, "I'm here to pump you up!" Let me hear you try! |

# OZ BEEN BORN AGAIN!

**Lion:** [boldly] I'm here to pump [becomes timid] y-y-your g-g-gas.

**Giz:** Oh well, close enough. How about you, little lady? What can I do for you?

**Dorothy:** I don't need your help! After all, you didn't help my friends. They needed a new heart, a new mind and a new nature. All you offered them was a new wardrobe—and a rather tacky one, I might add. Why didn't you take care of their real needs?

**Giz:** Hey...lay off, lady! Who do you think I am...God?

## DISCUSSION

1. How have you changed the most in the last year? What one thing about yourself do you hope never changes? Why? How have you changed most since becoming a Christian?

2. In what ways have you tried to make a huge lifestyle change on your own? What happened?

3. How did Giz's gifts to the characters in this skit make a change in their lives? Did the characters believe they had been changed? Why?

4. Read Romans 7:15-25. According to this passage, what happens when we try to make deep changes within ourselves on our own? Who can rescue us from this cycle of failure?

5. Read 2 Corinthians 3:12-18. Who is transforming us? What are we being transformed into? Is this a work that we are doing on our own?

6. What area of your life would you most like to see God transform? Why? From your heart, commit these areas to God right now. Ask Him to change you with His transforming power.

# CONTRADICTIONS

## TOPICS: CHRISTIAN LOVE, MESSAGES OUR LIVES SEND

### CHARACTERS
Bag Lady (preferably a guy)
Bridget (who always speaks loudly when addressing Bag Lady)
Janae
Gabriel
Jamal

### PROPS
Bench, garbage can, bird seed in bag, soda in can, magazine, backpack, Bible and paper bag.

*Bag Lady is sitting on a bench next to a garbage can in a park, feeding birds from a bag of seed. She occasionally takes a sip out of her paper bag.*

**Bag Lady:** Come here, little birdies. There you go. Share the seed now. *[shoos a bird away]* Seed hog! All the little ones need some, too! *[She talks to the birds as two students enter. They watch Bag Lady feed the birds and coax each other to sit down next to her.]*

**Janae:** *[whispers loudly]* Is it a man or woman?

**Bridget:** I have no idea. Have you ever noticed how you can never tell with these people?

**Janae:** I think it's a woman.

**Bridget:** *[yells into Bag Lady's ear]* Hello!

**Bag Lady:** *[shocked, falls of the bench]* Huh? Oh...

**Janae:** *[sips a soda]* I guess you didn't hear us.

**Bag Lady:** I guess not.

**Bridget:** Ah, listen, my name is Bridget, and this is Janae. We are so glad to meet you. *[tries to shake Bag Lady's hand]* Uh, this is a nice park, huh? *[Bag Lady keeps feeding the birds.]*

Page 26

# CONTRADICTIONS

**Janae:** Nice birds.

**Bridget:** Uh, yeah. *[pause, then to Bag Lady]* Wow, I can't imagine *me* living here!

**Janae:** *[pokes Bridget and whispers loudly]* Shut up! What if he/she lives here?

**Bridget:** What I meant to say is that this park is nice for certain people to live in I'm sure...skip it. Listen, we saw you sitting here and just wanted to come down and be your friends. Do you have any friends?

*[Bag Lady hesitates, then nods her head yes, but Janae just keeps on going.]*

**Janae:** Well, let us be your first friends.

**Bridget:** Speaking of friends, I would like to introduce you to Jesus Christ, my best friend. *[Bag Lady looks around for Bridget's friend]* Oh, no. He's not here. He lives in here, your heart. You see, when you accept Jesus Christ into your life, He becomes the most important part of your life. He changes everything.

**Janae:** *[cuts in]* Go ahead, tell her about God's love.

**Bridget:** I will. I will. God really loves you, you know. He sent His Son to die for you.

**Janae:** No! No! Tell her about God's love for her!

**Bridget:** *[impatiently]* Would you shut up? I'm trying. If you would stop flapping your big fat mouth, I could find some time to tell her about the love of God! *[sweetly to Bag Lady]* You see, as Christians, God's love is so evident anywhere you go! *[turns to Janae who has been tapping her constantly]* Do you mind? And get that stupid soda out of your hand—she probably is really thirsty and we aren't supposed to feed them until next week's outreach.

*[As Bridget grabs the soda, she overcompensates and spills it all over Bag Lady.]* Oh, I am so sorry. *[to Janae]* Look what you did now! *[Bridget continues talking while trying to dry off Bag Lady. Janae tries to help.]*

Sit down; I'll do this. You are such a dork. No, not you Bag Person, I mean... forget it. Where was I? Oh, yeah, Jesus comes and gets inside of your heart and takes over every part of who you are. You see, there is a sinful part of your life called your sinful nature.

# CONTRADICTIONS

**Janae:** Yeah, you know, I think Metallica sings a song about sin. Which CD is that anyway?

**Bridget:** Oh, never mind. It's not the type of music you listen to, but it's all in what you believe.

**Janae:** Isn't there a verse about that in the Bible?

**Bridget:** Yeah, it's right here. I think I brought a Bible with me. *[Looks in her bag, overcompensates to get it out. It hits Bag Lady in the face.]*

**Janae:** Are you OK? *[notices a magazine in the backpack]* Hey, what are you doing with that kind of magazine?

**Bridget:** *[hides it]* There is an article in here I was trying to read, all right?

**Janae:** Right. On what, your thought life?

**Bridget:** Listen, I don't need to take this from you, you jerk. Let's go! Right here. C'mon! *[starts to fight as Bag Lady tries to stop them]*

**Janae:** *[to Bag Lady]* Hey, what are you doing? We're the Christians!

**Bridget:** *[to Bag Lady]* Yeah, if we hadn't come down here to say anything to you, this would never have happened! So just sit down, relax and decide if you want Jesus Christ in your life or not!

**Janae:** Yeah, we are only going to give you one chance—we have no time to cast pearls before swine—oh, that's a Bible verse we can tell you about once you have Jesus in your heart and can understand the Bible.

*[Bridget and Janae continue to poke at each other, then break out in fighting again. A punch is thrown and Bag Lady is hit accidentally, which knocks her to the ground and out cold. The two students keep fighting.]*

**Bridget:** Oh no, look what you did!

**Janae:** ME? I was just hitting you back.

**Bridget:** Your mom is going to find out about this!

**Janae:** Mom?! Who gives a rip about what my mom thinks? I don't!

# CONTRADICTIONS

**Gabriel:** *[comes in with Jamal]* Hey, Hey! *[breaks up the fight]* What's going on here?

**Jamal:** Yeah, we were supposed to be out witnessing in the park today. This looks like a stunt out of WWF (World Wrestling Federation)!

**Bridget:** *[points to Bag Lady]* I was trying to show him/her the love of God and this imbecile... *[Jamal interrupts.]*

**Jamal:** How on earth did he/she get on the ground—facedown?

**Janae:** It was just the uhhhh power of God, I guess!

**Jamal:** Either that or he/she was hungry for some bird seed!

**Janae:** You think he/she accepted Jesus?

**Bridget:** I don't know how he/she couldn't have.

**Bridget:** Yeah, our lives really must have made a statement!

**Gabriel:** Come on, a bunch of us are tired of talking to street people. We're going to see a movie.

**Bridget and Janae:** All right! Let's go.

**Janae:** *[looks at Bag Lady]* Wait, what should we do with him/her?

**Bridget:** Nothing, I guess.

**Gabriel:** Let's go.

**Bridget:** God bless you!

*[They all leave Bag Lady alone. She wakes up, brushes herself off and begins feeding the birds again.]*

**Bag Lady:** *[sings the entire first verse of "Amazing Grace" and exits the stage]* Amazing grace, how sweet the sound...

# CONTRADICTIONS

## DISCUSSION

1. In what ways were Bridget and Janae not as loving toward this woman as they should have been? What did Bridget and Janae's actions and words say about them to this woman in the park? What did their behavior say about Jesus and a relationship with Him?

2. Someone has said, "Tell others about Christ, and if you must, use words." What does this mean to you?

3. Read Matthew 22:37-39; John 13:35; 1 Corinthians 13:1-3,13 and 1 John 4:7-12. What did Jesus say was the greatest commandment (Matt. 22:37-39)? Why do you think Jesus so closely intertwines our love for God with our love for others? What is to be the number one message of our lives to others?

4. Who are the people in your life you consider to be most loving? What are some things they do that cause you to feel loved?

5. In what ways are you most loving? In what ways have you found it difficult in the past to love others? In what ways would you like to be more loving?

6. What one thing will you do to begin to be more loving toward God? toward others?

# LONELY LARRY LEBANOWSKI

## TOPIC: LONELINESS

**CHARACTER**

Larry

**NOTE**

Larry's delivery at the beginning of the monologue should be light-hearted and sarcastic. His delivery should darken as the drama proceeds but end with a cautiously hopeful tone.

**PROPS**

Couch, notebook journal and piece of fancy stationery.

## SCENE 1

*Larry enters, looking for his family.*

Larry: Mom? Mom, I'm home. Mom? Mom. *[yelling louder]* Mom. Dad? Dad. Katie? Katie. Panda. Come here, girl. Panda? Where is everybody? Great, I'm alone again. *[pause]* Fine. It's OK. I can be alone. It's past 10 o'clock. I'm home. I'll just read my note from Jennifer—again. *[throws himself down on sofa, pulls out fancily-folded note and reads aloud]*

*Dear Larry,*

*I'm sorry to tell you this in a note, but you know how I can't handle uncomfortable situations. First, I just want to say that I will always love you. The last five months have been really special. And you know I think you're cute, especially your nose.*

*[drops note and talks back to Jennifer]*

Oh, Jennifer, do you mean the "monolith on Larry's face," as you referred to it to your friend Stacy?

*[picks up the note]*

*I don't know how else to say it. I don't want to "go with" you anymore. There's no one else, so it's not about that.*

Page 31

# LONELY LARRY LEBANOWSKI

*[again speaks to Jennifer]*

Of course there's no one else, Jennifer, including Glenn who walked you to every class today and kissed you goodbye. Glenn, my best friend until today. Glenn, who also has a big nose.

*[refers back to the note]*

*And it's got nothing to do with you, you're the best. This is all about me. I just need some space, some time to myself. Someone once said "If you love something, set it free. If it returns to you, it is yours to keep. If it doesn't it was never meant to be."*

*Love (as a friend) always,*

*Jennifer*

*[sadly]* Well, Jennifer, thank you for setting me free. I'll be fine, all alone in my house at 10 o'clock, with no girlfriend, no best friend and no family. I'll be just...fine.

*[aloud to himself]* Why do I have no friends? I'm a nice guy. What am I saying—I've got friends. I'm pretty popular with....um...lots of people.

*[pause]* OK, God, I need you to be my only friend right now. OK? I've got my journal here. *[gets up, picks up journal from beside the couch and begins leafing through it]* How can I be lonely? God is with me, so I'm never really alone. I'm not lonely anymore cause I've got God. *[Singing]* "'Cause I've got God. 'Cause I've got God, God, God. You're my friend. You're my friend." *[Regaining his composure]* OK, I'll be quiet...but I **feel** very alone.

So God, I'm just gonna write in my journal because then I won't be lonely *[talking continuously]* because I'm not lonely because I've got my journal and I've got You. OK, here it goes. OK.

*[speaks aloud as he writes in his journal]*

*Dear God,*

*I'm saying "dear" because You are dear to me, and You're a friend. Um, as You know, Jennifer broke up with me today, and I'm very lonely right now. In fact, I'm probably at the brink of tears. But, that's OK 'cause I don't need girls anyway 'cause they have problems, and I am a man and I don't have any. Well, let me continue. Father, who art in heaven, how will it be thy name.*

*[laughs at his own joke]*

# LONELY LARRY LEBANOWSKI

O.K. I want You to know that my mom and dad aren't here right now, and neither is my dog. I don't know where she is. Actually, she was neutered and she is really a he, but for some reason I call him a her.

Well, I guess what I'm trying to say is that, um, I'm trying to act like I'm not really lonely, but I really am. My girlfriend is gone, my best friend is gone, my family is gone. God, I have **nobody**!

I mean, what did I do tonight? I worked on my geometry exam **alone** for four hours and just got back from Burger King where I ate **alone**. I mean, I'm an adult here, and I've got nobody.

Well, I'm getting a little bitter here. Do You hear me? Bitter, B-I-T-T-E-R. I'm getting angry because if I'm gonna be lonely my whole life, well, I don't know how much life is actually worth living. I know I'm supposed to live for You, but sometimes it's just lonely.

Tonight I just feel really lonely. And because of that, I'm gonna get out of this journal entry and go mope around. Maybe I'll cry. I'll listen to a really sad song but, God, help me.

*[Lights fade out. Larry goes offstage.]*

## SCENE 2

*Again Larry enters, looking for his family.*

Larry: Um, Mom? Mom. Dad? Dad. Katie? Panda? OK, two days in a row. The only difference is that tonight is my birthday. As a matter of fact, it's my eighteenth birthday. It's my birthday, and nobody's home to celebrate it with me. Well, so what? I'm gonna have my own birthday celebration. *[He flops onto the couch and humorously breaks into several birthday songs. He ends with "Nobody knows the trouble I've seen..."]* It's my birthday, God, and I didn't even get a present yet. Forget it. It's nobody else's birthday in the world but mine, and nobody remembered it. Well, You know what? I'm gonna write You a birthday gift. Yeah, that's what I'm gonna do.

*[grabs his journal from beside the sofa]*

# LONELY LARRY LEBANOWSKI

Dear God,

It's my birthday today, but You already knew that, didn't You? Every hair on my lonely head is numbered. I just wondered if You knew 'cause uh, nobody's here to celebrate it with me. Every day of my life was ordained by You. So I guess You knew a long time ago that I would be alone right now, on my birthday. My eighteenth birthday.

OK, OK, instead of taking this time and complaining about being alone, God, I guess for the first time I'll take my aloneness and give it to You. I guess I could call it my alone time—with You, right? Ha, ha, ha. OK... I'm turning **18** and nobody's around. So, nobody's around to celebrate one of the biggest days of my life. In fact, no one has even mentioned it.

Maybe they don't know. Maybe they forgot. Maybe I don't want to know. So, I didn't get the presents I wanted. So, no girl called me tonight and told me that I was a hot stud...and I am. Somebody will find that out someday. Even so, I'm gonna make it, because, You know what, I'm gonna take my lonely times and make them alone times with You.

So, the world thinks I'm ugly. So, my nose is too big. So, my feet smell. It's OK because You still love me, and I'm gonna take this time, and I'm gonna do something with it.

There were other people in the Bible who were alone, too. David was alone. Paul was alone. And, well, the disciples after You died were alone. They felt it, too, and they didn't give up, and so I won't either. No way! I'm gonna make my alone times special. I'm gonna give them all to You. You know what, God? I think that You think I'm pretty good—and I am. Well, I guess what I'm trying to say is...I can even be alone with You and be OK because You still love me. Thanks, God. Thanks for letting me be alone. Hold me close.

Love, Larry

# LONELY LARRY LEBANOWSKI

## DISCUSSION

1. What was going on with Larry? Did he seem to enjoy being alone? How did he react at first? Why do you think he finally turned his loneliness over to God?

2. Which do you most prefer, being alone or being with a crowd? Why? Is loneliness a good thing or a bad thing? Why?

3. Read Psalm 142. What did David, who wrote this psalm while in a cave, have in common with Larry? How did David react to his loneliness?

4. When have you felt most alone? Why? How did you handle it? How could you have handled it differently?

5. Let's brainstorm a list of things we could do during lonely times to be sure they are positive and constructive. *(List suggestions on a chalkboard or have group members take notes on this.)*

6. Decide right now what you will do the next time you are lonely. How will you turn it over to God and pour your heart out to Him?

# ONE CHRISTIAN FITS ALL

## TOPICS: ACCEPTANCE, FRIENDLINESS, GROUP BUILDING

### CHARACTERS
Josh (visitor dressed normally with baggy pants; speaks in a normal voice)
Ralph (youth group member dressed in "high water" baggy pants, suspenders, thick glasses, pocket protector and slicked back hair; speaks in a nasal, irritating voice)
Jesus (dressed in robe and sandals)

### PROPS
Suspenders, thick glasses with nose bridge taped and clothespin.

*Josh enters. He is approached by Ralph, who offers a handshake.*

**Josh:** *[shakes Ralph's hand]* Hi. I'm Josh.

**Ralph:** Hi, Josh. How are you doing today?

**Josh:** To be quite honest, I'm a little nervous about visiting the youth group. I can't help wondering if I will fit in.

**Ralph:** Oh, Josh, don't be silly! *[snorts as he laughs]* At our youth group we love and accept everyone just as they are. You'll fit in just perfectly. That is, except for...oh well, forget it!

**Josh:** Forget what? It's my breath, isn't it? *[cups hand, breathes into it and sniffs]* I knew I shouldn't have had those garlic nacho cheese puffs before I came.

**Ralph:** Oh, no...that's not it at all. I love the smell of cheese.

**Josh:** Then what is it?

**Ralph:** Please understand that it doesn't make any difference to us how you dress, mind you. However, I must admit that your choice in fashion is...might I say... C-average or below. *[snorts as he laughs]*

**Josh:** Gee, all I want to do is fit in. Do you think you can help me?

# ONE CHRISTIAN FITS ALL

**Ralph:** It won't be easy...but at this church we do believe in miracles. Hmmm, let me see what we can do first. *[scratches head]* Aaaaaah yes...I've got it! The first thing you need to do in order to take on the glorious appearance of *moi* (mwah) is to do a slight trouser height readjustment. You see...your trousers are close to the world. We like our trousers to reach up to the heavens, like so. *[pulls at his trousers]*

**Josh:** Oh, I see. *[pulls up on his trousers until they can go no further]* Is this better?

**Ralph:** You look marvelous...I can only think of one more thing that might help you fit in, if you know what I mean. *[snorts as he laughs]*

**Josh:** I am willing to do anything to fit in with the youth group. What is it that I need to do?

**Ralph:** It just so happens that I carry with me an extra pair of suspenders. You never know when you might run into an unexpected elastic emergency. You are more than welcome to use them. *[pulls out ugly, wide suspenders]*

**Josh:** Oh, thank you so very, very much. I don't know what to say. *[puts on suspenders]*

**Ralph:** It's obvious that you don't know what to say. Perhaps I could be of some assistance in this matter as well. I don't mean to be critical—you know that this church is anything but critical. However, if you ask me, your voice is a little...can we say...irritating. Where in the world did you get such a voice anyhow?

**Josh:** I was born with this voice.

**Ralph:** Don't worry, at this church we will never hold that against you. However, you might consider a more appealing vocal quality...perhaps you might mimic my superior voice tone and pitch.

**Josh:** Please show me how.

**Ralph:** *[pulls out clothespin and clips it on nose]* I think that this will do just fine. Come on now, give it a try. Why don't you say something like, "Do you have any cheese?"

**Josh:** *[in new voice]* Do you have any cheese?

**Ralph:** That's almost perfect!

# ONE CHRISTIAN FITS ALL

**Josh:** What do you mean, *almost* perfect?

**Ralph:** I was thinking that perhaps some glasses might help you take on an appearance of biblical authority.

**Josh:** But I don't know anything about the Bible.

**Ralph:** Oh, don't let that bother you. No one in this youth group knows anything about the Bible either. All that matters is that you look like you do. Here, put these on. *[hands him thick glasses with tape in middle]* Now that is wonderful! Just remember to raise your hands during any slow songs.

**Josh:** You mean like this? *[holds hands half way up]*

**Ralph:** Oh, no....like this! *[holds hands very high in air]* Then it doesn't hurt to sway back and forth like a tree in the wind!

**Josh:** Like this? *[attempts with vigorous side-to-side motion]*

**Ralph:** I said sway like a tree in the wind, not like a washing machine on spin. Here, try this. *[puts arms really high in the air]* Oh, yes...if all else fails, it helps to do this. *[grabs Josh's head and forces it to side]* Yes...that's it. Now bat your eyelashes like you have a speck in your eye or something.

**Josh:** *[attempts]* Is this good?

**Ralph:** Now that is absolutely wonderful. Don't worry about a thing. At our youth group we accept people just the way they are. You're going to fit in just fine. Just say an occasional hallelujah, and go into the youth room and sit anywhere you wish. That is, of course, except for my seat.

**Josh:** Thank you so much. I feel so much more comfortable now. *[exits waving hands, snorting, saying hallelujah, wearing new garb]*

**Ralph:** *[with big smile on his face]* Needs a **lot** of work, but he'll probably be OK here.

*[Jesus enters and approaches Ralph.]*

**Ralph:** Welcome to our youth group!

**Jesus:** I am just visiting your youth group today, and to be quite honest with you, I was wondering if I am going to fit in.

# ONE CHRISTIAN FITS ALL

**Ralph:** Don't you worry about a thing. At this church we still believe in miracles. However, with you it might take a little bit more work than with others. But...I still think we can do something to help you fit in.

**Jesus:** [*disappointed*] That's what I was afraid of.

## DISCUSSION

1. Was Josh really accepted by Ralph? Why? What did Ralph say that was right? How did his actions contradict what he said?

2. How have you experienced difficulty finding acceptance with a certain crowd or in a church youth group? Tell us about it. How has this experience affected how accepting you are of people new to our group?

3. Why is it important that church youth groups accept anyone—without prejudice or conditions?

4. Read Luke 7:18-23. From what you know of Jesus, why might John have had some doubt of whether or not Jesus was the Messiah? What might he have expected? Had John not accepted Jesus, on what would he have missed out?

5. Jesus knew people might be offended by His personality or characteristics (v. 23). What personality traits or attitudes in others do you have a difficult time accepting? Why?

6. If everyone in our youth group suddenly became more accepting of one another, what effect would it have on you? on others in the group? on people new to our group or visitors?

7. What one thing can you do to be more accepting of new people or visitors to our group?

# JENNY'S SIN

## TOPICS: FORGIVENESS, RESPONSE TO A CHRISTIAN WHO SINS

### CHARACTERS
Jenny
Lori
Kendrick
Viv
Annie
Carlos
Amy
Person distributing fliers

### PROPS
Four chairs, book, schoolbooks, Bible purse, large binoculars and basketball. Place two chairs stage left for Viv and Annie. Place two chairs at center stage for Jenny.

*Jenny is center stage on her knees, with her elbows on the seat of a chair. Audience sees her profile as she prays.*

**Jenny:** Lord, I know I should have come to You a long time ago about this, and I am truly sorry. Please forgive me for what I've done and help me through this. And please help me as I go to those I've hurt and ask them for their forgiveness. Thank You, Lord, for forgiving me. Amen.

*[Jenny stands, turns the chair around and sits down, closing her eyes and sighing with relief. Lori walks in from the right carrying a big Bible, stopping when she notices Jenny. Lori feels uncomfortable talking to Jenny.]*

**Lori:** Um...Uh...Hi, Jenny.

**Jenny:** Hey, Lori...Why are you looking at me funny?

**Lori:** Funny? I'm sorry I didn't realize I was doing that. It's just...

**Jenny:** Just what?

# JENNY'S SIN

**Lori:** Look, I just didn't expect to see you here at youth group.

**Jenny:** So you heard about what I did, huh?

**Lori:** *[frankly]* Jenny, my granny heard about what you did.

**Jenny:** *[surprised]* Mee-Maw?

**Lori:** I'm afraid so.

**Jenny:** How'd she find out?

**Lori:** Do the words **worldwide web** mean anything to you?

*[Jenny covers her face with her hands.]*

**Lori:** *[looking for an escape]* Well, I need to...um...run home real quick. I forgot to feed my...uh...snake this morning. I'll see you later, Jenny, but look, umm, don't let anyone else know I spoke with you, OK?

**Jenny:** *[dryly]* Your dastardly little secret is safe with me.

**Lori:** Oh, you're such a good...

**Jenny:** Friend?

*[Lori shakes her head, then shrugs, giggles nervously and hurries quickly away, looking over her shoulder as she leaves. Jenny pulls a book out of her pocket and begins to read. Kendrick walks in from stage right dribbling a basketball, stopping when he recognizes Jenny.]*

**Kendrick:** Hey, aren't you the girl who...

**Jenny:** *[quickly interrupting]* Yeah, that was me. Aren't you the guy who mindlessly dribbles his basketball everywhere he goes? I'm sorry, I'm having a rough day.

**Kendrick:** A man's got to practice to keep his game on—you know what I'm saying?

**Jenny:** Whatever.

**Kendrick:** I mean, it's important to always do what we know is right, to always do our best, to strive for perfection...you know what I mean?

# JENNY'S SIN

**Jenny:** Yes, I think I do.

**Kendrick:** So, what are you doing here?

**Jenny:** What do you mean?

**Kendrick:** I mean, how can you just show up here—at the church?

**Jenny:** What's that supposed to mean?

**Kendrick:** If it were me, I'd be too embarrassed. I mean, if everyone knew what I did. And I mean **everyone**.

**Jenny:** Here? At church?

**Kendrick:** *[nodding his head]* Oh, yeah.

**Jenny:** The youth group?

**Kendrick:** *[nodding more]* Ohhhh, yeah, yeah, yeah.

**Jenny:** *[timidly]* What did they say?

**Kendrick:** *[shaking his head emphatically]* Ohhhh, no, no, no.

**Jenny:** Come on. You can tell me.

**Kendrick:** You still have time to sneak out before everyone gets here.

**Jenny:** Why would I do that?

**Kendrick:** You don't have much time. For your own sake, start sneaking.

*[Jenny's jaw drops in unbelief. Kendrick dribbles his basketball as he exits stage left. Jenny continues to read her book as Viv enters from stage left. She stops dead in her tracks, about 15 feet away from Jenny. Viv bends over and squints, trying to determine if the girl is Jenny. She tiptoes a few feet closer, leans over and squints some more. Annie, carrying a purse, approaches from stage left and stands behind Viv. Annie leans over right beside Viv, who doesn't even notice her.]*

**Annie:** What are you doing?

# JENNY'S SIN

**Viv:** *[startled, screams as she flails her arms in the air]* You scared me to death.

*[Jenny looks over in their direction but resumes her reading.]*

**Annie:** Who is that?

**Viv:** I think it's Jenny.

**Annie:** Jenny? You mean the girl who—

**Viv:** *[interrupting]* The one and only.

**Annie:** Hold on a second.

*[Annie pulls out a huge pair of binoculars from her purse, puts the strap around her neck, and tries to focus on Jenny.]*

**Annie:** Yep. It's Jenny.

*[Jenny notices them and smiles as she waves to them. Still looking toward Jenny, the two spies slowly raise a weak wave. Jenny continues to read.]*

**Annie:** I think she sees us.

*[Annie turns to Viv and gives her a cowardly expression. Viv replies with a fake smile. Annie lowers the binoculars.]*

**Annie:** She might have seen us, but she doesn't know who we are. We're too far away.

*[Viv sits down beside Annie. Jenny continues to read.]*

**Viv:** But how do I get in the church behind her without her seeing me? I'd really like to avoid her if I could.

**Annie:** I thought she was your friend.

**Viv:** She is. But it would be too weird. I wouldn't know what to say.

**Annie:** I've got an idea. Follow me.

# JENNY'S SIN

[*Annie stands up and pretends to see a bird in the direction of the audience. She points it out to Viv. Annie looks through the binoculars and pretends to see the bird. With their backs to Jenny, the two girls shuffle across the stage directly in front of her, continuing to pass the binoculars between them as they both point toward the imaginary bird. Jenny watches them and shakes her head in disbelief as they exit stage right. Jenny then continues to read her book.*

*Carlos, carrying a Bible, enters with a confident stride from stage right. Jenny watches him as he methodically stops beside Jenny, stands straight, clears his throat and points at her. He then shouts at Jenny as he continues to point at her.*]

**Carlos:** [*shouting*] Sinnnnnerrrrrrrr!!

[*Carlos exits with nose in the air. Jenny shakes head in disbelief, but continues reading as Amy walks in from stage left, carrying a load of schoolbooks.*]

**Amy:** Hi, Jenny.

**Jenny:** [*dejected*] Hey, Amy.

**Amy:** You mind if I sit down?

**Jenny:** Of course not.

[*Amy sits in the chair beside Jenny.*]

**Jenny:** You're actually talking to me?

**Amy:** Yeah. Why wouldn't I?

**Jenny:** You don't know about the terrible thing I did, do you?

**Amy:** Of course.

**Jenny:** How did you find out?

**Amy:** Are you kidding? We've got cable.

**Jenny:** What was I thinking?

**Amy:** Well, I want you to know that if you need anything, I'm here for you.

# JENNY'S SIN

**Jenny:** *[sadly]* You're the only one.

**Amy:** Why do you say that?

**Jenny:** Everyone's treating me like I have the plague—like I've committed some unpardonable sin. And they're supposed to be my Christian brothers and sisters.

**Amy:** I'm sorry.

**Jenny:** It's not your fault. It's theirs.

*[Person walks by distributing fliers. Amy and Jenny both take one.]*

**Amy:** Don't let them get to you. It's most important to focus on what God thinks about you right now. He forgives and forgets. *[pauses to read the flier]*

Oh, look at this. There's been a last-minute change in the theme of tonight's youth service. Instead of "Five Steps to Bringing a Heathen to God," we'll be talking about "Sin in the Camp." Wow! That's...strange.

**Jenny:** *[head in hands]* Not really.

# JENNY'S SIN

## DISCUSSION

1. What do you think was Jenny's sin? Does it really matter what she did? Does committing certain sins justify mistreatment by others? Why?

2. Jenny had already asked God to forgive her and for His help to get her back on track. If the group members who shunned her had known this, do you think their reactions would have been different? Should this matter or not?

3. What did Amy do right in how she reacted to Jenny and her sin? What else could she have done?

4. Think of something bad you have done and how people reacted to you when they found out about it. Without mentioning what you did, recall the kinds of reactions you got from people. What is your most vivid recollection of what people did and said? How do you wish people would have reacted? Why?

5. Read Psalms 32:4-7; 103:11-13; Ephesians 4:32 and 2 Timothy 4:16-18. What can we learn about God's forgiveness and our responsibility to forgive others from these verses? What encouragement can we find in these verses when we fall into sin or make mistakes?

6. Is there anyone you have judged, rejected or mistreated due to their sin? Take time right now to forgive that person from your heart and to seek your own forgiveness. Consider what God may have you say to that person.

7. From all we have discussed today, what one thing will you be sure to do next time you hear of a brother or sister who has sinned? What will you do to help him be restored? to protect him from mistreatment by others?

# SCRIPTURE IN A CAN

## TOPICS: THE BIBLE, POWER OF THE WORD

## Characters
Demon
Melissa
Arnie
Announcer

## Props
Athletic ball pump, victorious music cassette, cassette player, spray can (of air freshener) labeled "Scripture in a Can" and cafeteria tray filled with food.

## SCENE 1

*Melissa stands by innocently as Demon sneaks up.*

Demon: Well, hello there, and how are you today?

Melissa: I'm just fine.

Demon: Oh, that's sad—I mean good—to hear; however, I have a feeling you won't be feeling well soon.

Melissa: Why do you say that?

Demon: Because I am the demon of sickness and disease, and I am going to attack you and steal away your health!

Melissa: I don't think so! You have overlooked the fact that I've had my booster shots, my tetanus shots, my chicken pox vaccine, my mumps vaccine, my polio vaccine—and to top it all off, I had my teeth cleaned this morning.

Demon: Ahhh yes, but I think you have forgotten to protect yourself against this! *[pulls out ball pump and uses like hypodermic needle to Melissa's toe]* **Main toe poisoning!**

# SCRIPTURE IN A CAN

**Melissa:** *[screams and grabs foot as she jumps around]* Somebody help me...please...call a tow truck!

**Demon:** There is no hope for you. There isn't a single pill, potion or tow truck that can help you now!

**Melissa:** Then I will go to a podiatrist and have surgery. Surely the doctor can help.

**Demon:** There is no hope for you. There isn't a single po-, po- po- *[stutters]*...oh, you know...a foot doctor can't help! There is no hope for you.

**Melissa:** You mean...I'm gonna die because of main toe poisoning? *[gasps and begins dying a corny, dramatic death]*

**Announcer:** Has something like this ever happened to you? Well, it never has to again as long as you have "Scripture in a Can"!

*["Rewind" and replay Melissa and Demon just before Demon attacked.]*

**Demon:** There is no hope for you. I am going to give you main toe poisoning!

*[Play victory music.]*

**Melissa:** Not so fast, you foul pagan scum! I have "Scripture in a Can"!

**Demon:** Oh, no...not "Scripture in a Can"!

**Melissa:** It says right here on the label that you are defeated because it is by Christ's wounds that we have been healed, 1 Peter 2 dot dot 24. *[Pretends to spray Demon—sound effects and all. Demon drops in sudden death as Melissa lifts hands in victory.]*

## SCENE 2

*Arnie is approached by the same Demon.*

**Demon:** I have come to destroy you. I am the demon of fear!

**Arnie:** *[shudders every time fear is mentioned]* I'm sorry, but I don't believe in fear. *[shudders]*

**Demon:** Oh, yeah? Then how do you explain this? Knock, Knock.

# SCRIPTURE IN A CAN

**Arnie:** Who's there?

**Demon:** Boo! *[laughs]*

**Arnie:** Boo-hoo! Please stop! There is no hope for me! My heart is gripped with fear. *[shudders]*

**Demon:** There is one last thing I want you to fear. *[Arnie shudders.]*

**Arnie:** W-w-what is it?

**Demon:** It's the scariest thing you have ever laid your eyes upon. It's the... *[brings out cafeteria tray with food]*

**Arnie:** Oh, no...not the school lunch! *[screams and begins dying a dramatic death]*

**Announcer:** Has this situation ever happened to you? Perhaps you got a little nervous while singing your solo at choir rehearsal. *[Arnie shudders.]* Well, never again, as long as you have "Scripture in a Can"!

*["Rewind" and replay Arnie and Demon just before Demon attacked.]*

**Demon:** I have come to destroy you with fear!

**Arnie:** I don't think so, you demon of fear! *[dramatically holds up can]* I have come prepared with "Scripture in a Can"!

**Demon:** *[shudders]* Oh, no—not "Scripture in a Can"!

**Arnie:** Yes. "Scripture in a Can"! It says right here on the label that you are already defeated. "The Lord is my light and my salvation—whom shall I fear?" Psalm 27 dot dot 1. *[Pretends to spray Demon—sound effects and all. Demon, does a "dying roach" dramatic death.]*

**Announcer:** Don't struggle through another day without "Scripture in a Can"! Never again will you be defeated by the attacks of your enemy. The cost is absolutely free (however, prices may vary slightly in California and New York). Don't write to Spiegel catalog. Don't look for it in your next box of Sugar Puffs. Just ask your Lord and Savior, and remember the words of the Psalmist, "Your Word have I hid in my heart, that I might not sin against You."

# SCRIPTURE IN A CAN

## DISCUSSION

1. What is the most impressive display of power you have ever seen anywhere (i.e., volcanic eruption, hurricane, nuclear explosion, etc.)? How do you remember feeling as you witnessed it?

2. In this skit, how did Melissa and Arnie's attitudes change when they had "Scripture in a Can"? What was realistic about the power of "Scripture in a Can"? What was unrealistic?

3. Read Psalm 119:89-96. What power does God's Word possess? What benefits does this hold for our lives? Why? How do you think the psalmist gained such a fondness for God's Word—so much that he declares that he "delights" in it?

4. What does verse 96 mean to you?

5. What one thing will you do to more "delight" in God's Word? In what one way do you most need to see the power of God's Word at work in your life? Why? What verse can you recall that would be good to remember well during this time as you pray for the power of God's Word in your life?

# OUT FROM THE COLD AND INTO THE BOLD

## TOPICS: BOLDNESS, RISK-TAKING, BEING A DOER OF THE WORD

### CHARACTERS

Youth Leader
Bill (always has his Bible with him)
Renee
Kelly
Seth
Woman 1
Child
Mime
Friend
Man 1
Woman 2
Man 2

### PROPS

Four bags of "groceries," beach ball, "beer" can and wooden door with door frame (can be imaginary).

## SCENE 1

*Youth Leader stands stage left facing Bill, Renee, Kelly and Seth, who are standing stage right. Everyone is pumped up and excited.*

**Youth Leader:** I said, "Seize the opportunity to bring them to Jesus!"

**Girls, Seth, Bill:** *[jump up and down, excitedly cheering, clapping and yelling "Amen!"]*

**Youth Leader:** You can change the world!

**Girls, Seth, Bill:** *[cheer, clap, yell]*

# OUT FROM THE COLD AND INTO THE BOLD

**Youth Leader:** Bow your heads and let's pray. How many of you would say tonight that you are ready to do anything God asks?

**Girls, Seth, Bill:** *[shakes heads in agreement, raises hand and closes eyes]* We're Yours, Lord!

**Renee:** *[lifts head in alarm]* Wait a minute. Anything? What if He asks me to do something I don't like? What if He sends me to, like, Borneo or something? Hmmm. *[looks around and does an exaggerated tiptoe exit]*

**Youth Leader:** How many would say, "I'm tired of living average, watered-down Christianity. I'm gonna be bold for God!"?

**Kelly, Seth, Bill:** *[yell]* We're going to be bold for You, Lord! *[pantomime excitement]*

**Kelly:** *[places hands on hair and smacks on imaginary gum]* Bald for God?! *[giggles]* Uhh...I love God and everything, but no way am I gonna be **bald** for Him. *[looks at Seth and Bill, then quietly slides out of the room]*

**Youth Leader:** How many would say, "I'm going to be a powerful witness for God, sharing Jesus with everyone I meet?"

**Seth and Bill:** *[excited and out of control yelling]* Yes, Lord! Yes, Lord! *[Bill continues, pantomiming his excitement as Seth speaks.]*

**Seth:** *[stops and looks thoughtful]* Hold on! If I commit to sharing Christ with everyone, that means I have to share Him with Butch, the biggest, baddest, meanest guy in school. So, I witness to Butch...he kills me...I'm martyred for my faith. I don't think so. Bye.

*[Seth turns and leaves. Bill stands alone and looks left, right and then hopefully to Youth Leader.]*

**Youth Leader:** *[checks watch]* Gee, you know, Bill, I'm sorry more people didn't join us in our commitment. I'd uhhhh...like to stay and pray with you about your commitment, but I've...uhh...got to get home and watch my favorite TV show. Look, just stay here as long as you need to and tell me what happens. God bless! Gotta go!

**Bill:** Hmmmph. *[looks around, looks up to God, not sure what to do, checks watch]* Never mind, Lord. *[leaves]*

# OUT FROM THE COLD AND INTO THE BOLD

## SCENE 2

*Bill is at center stage, reading Bible and praying.*

**Bill:** Oh, God, I love You with all my heart! I know You want to do big things in my life. What big things do You have for me to do? Anything, Lord—I'll do anything for You!

*[Woman 1 staggers by holding four bags of groceries. Bill sees her. Woman 1 smiles hopefully.]*

Here, let me help! *[Bill bends down and clears an imaginary stick from Woman 1's path.]* There, that stick's out of your way!

*[Woman 1 scowls and staggers on, shaking her head as Bill goes back to seeking God. Suddenly a beach ball rolls up to Bill's feet.]*

**Child:** *[yells to Bill, who is preoccupied]* Little help! Hey buddy, can you get my ball? Please? *[walks up to Bill and angrily snatches his ball]* Thanks a lot!

**Bill:** *[looking up happily]* Oh, umm, glad I could help!

*[Child walks off shaking head.]*

Lord, I just know You have big plans for me. Why won't You show me?

*[Mime comes out and improvises walking on a tightrope, then drops to his knees in front of Bill and gestures to show that his heart is broken and he needs the Bible Bill holds. When Mime touches the Bible, Bill misunderstands and becomes angry.]*

Hey, beat it, pal.

*[Bill pushes Mime, but Mime springs back. Bill and Mime push and shove, each time Mime comically springs back. Finally, Mime gestures angrily and leaves, holding his broken heart.]*

Good grief!...I'll do anything, Lord. Show me what You want me to do.

*[Friend enters, gives Bill complicated handshake.]*

**Friend:** Bill, I've been thinking about what you told me the other day about Jesus, and I think I'm ready to...

Page 53

## OUT FROM THE COLD AND INTO THE BOLD

**Bill:** Wait a minute. I don't mean to be rude, and I hope you'll understand this, but you see God is about to show me something big and important that I'm supposed to do. So, if you don't mind...

**Friend:** Oh...umm..sure. It was nothing anyway. *[leaves]*

**Bill:** Speak to me, Lord. Show me Your will.

## SCENE 3

*Bill is at center stage walking toward door, which is set up on stage facing the audience. Bill's back is to the audience.*

**Bill:** OK, Lord, I'm steppin' out for You. I'm gonna change my world; I'm gonna be all that I can be! Help me reach this poor, wretched, lost sinner with Your love. *[Knocks on door. Man 1 answers door, holding beer can and belching.]* Uh...hello sir, uh, I mean *[fire-and-brimstone-evangelist voice]*, sinner friend! The fiery, eternal pain and torment of hell await you unless you know Jesus. Do you know Jesus? *[Man 1 belches again and slams door in Bill's face.]*

What? Man, I blew it! *[brightens]* But I'm gonna change my world! I'm gonna be radical for God! *[walks away, then walks back as if walking to a different door]* OK, Lord, let me use my "Instant Convert" evangelism training for this next one...no mercy...I'm gonna change my world. *[He walks up to door and knocks. Door opens and Woman 2 "floats" out and around Bill as she speaks.]*

**Woman 2:** Ooohhh, helloooo. Isn't it a beautiful, wonderful day to become one with nature...to explore one's inner self...to float up and find one's origin in the cosmos...to coddle one's inner child...?

**Bill:** *[forcefully, yet mechanically as if reading]* Umm, Miss, if you were to walk in the street right now, get hit by a Mack truck and have yourself splattered all over the road, would you go to heaven and why do you say this? *[Woman 2 looks aghast, begins sniffling, hurries inside and slams the door shut. Bill shakes his head in disbelief and frustration as he walks away from the door.]*

God, what is going on? I'm trying to be a world changer. I'm trying to make a difference, and I blow it every time! I give up! Well, hmmm. One more, Lord? Why not? I'm into pain and rejection. *[He walks up to door and knocks. Man 2 answers.]*

# OUT FROM THE COLD AND INTO THE BOLD

                Hello, sir, my name is Bill. I'm a Christian, so kill me, abuse me, insult me—I can handle it. *[Man 2's mouth drops open, and he looks at Bill in disbelief.]*

**Man 2:**     I can't believe it. You actually came! God **does** exist, God **did** hear my prayer! Can you tell me how to have a personal relationship with God?

**Bill:**     *[puzzled]* Wait a second; it's not supposed to work like...Umm, sure, umm, let's look here in Romans. *[Bill opens Bible. Bill and Man 2 freeze.]*

## DISCUSSION

1. What hindrances to boldness and obedience to God did Bill experience in Scene 1? Scene 2? How was Bill taking a risk and being bold for God in Scene 3? Why did he almost quit? How did his boldness finally pay off?

2. In your opinion, what has God asked Christians to do that you feel requires the most risk? Why? What is the riskiest thing God has ever asked you to do?

3. What is the riskiest, boldest thing you have ever done for God? Why did you do it? How did it benefit you at the time? How has it benefitted you in the long term?

4. Read Acts 9:32-43. Picture yourself in Peter's place. What are you feeling? What are you thinking? What do you choose to do? What were all the results of Peter's risky prayer?

5. What holds you back from being a risk-taker or being more boldly obedient to God? What one bold action will you take for God?

# DEFENDER OR PRETENDER?

## TOPICS: COURAGE, STANDING UP FOR WHAT YOU BELIEVE

### CHARACTERS
Tim (Christian incognito, lacks courage to stand up for what he believes)
Ed (non-Christian friend)
Chris (Christian taking a stand for what he believes)
Sanders (the one who is questioning Chris)
Teacher

### PROPS
Bible (for Chris), briefcase, table and chair (for Teacher); chairs for class, cassette recording of a class bell and cassette player.

*The scene opens with Teacher set up at stage right quietly preparing himself for class, looking through papers. Chris and Sanders are sitting on or standing by their chairs and pantomime animated discussion throughout the sketch. Chris is holding a Bible. Both turn through it and look at it from time to time. Tim and Ed enter stage left. It is important that the audience see both their faces very clearly.*

**Tim:** *[making guitar solo sounds]* Du-nu-nu-duh-nunu-nah-nah-weeeer-wah! And then the drums kick in. *[makes drum solo sounds]* It was so cool—it blew away their last concert! Those guys rock. I love those guys. They are the greatest of all time!

**Ed:** The greatest? Give me a break! Then tell me this. How long has it been since you've heard any of their songs on the radio?

**Tim:** Radio? That doesn't mean anything. Have you heard the final cut on their last album? No! The lyrics alone put your band to shame.

**Ed:** Please! No way, man. Those guys lost it when they got that new guitarist, eh, what's-his-name?

**Tim:** Man, Sammy Nicks smokes any of those pretty boys you listen to! He's got technique, but he just goes from the gut! *[makes guitar solo sounds]* Wah-wah-du-nu-nu-nu-nah! I'm tellin' you, nobody touches that!

# DEFENDER OR PRETENDER?

**Ed:** I don't know, Tim.

**Tim:** I do. Shoot, you probably pick teams the way you pick your bands.

**Ed:** Hey, Redskins rule.

**Tim:** Redskins? Uh-uh! My Cowboys rule any day.

**Ed:** Hah. Not last week.

**Tim:** Don't you talk about the Cowboys, man! My team is comin' back hard—no mercy. My team! I'm talkin' about the best in the league. My team!

**Ed:** Your team?

**Tim:** Hey, man, I gotta defend 'em when I hear trash talk.

**Ed:** *[becomes distracted]* Look at that. "Chris the Christian" is cracking me up. *[gestures toward Chris and Sanders.]*

**Tim:** Huh?

*[Ed's gesture draws Chris' attention. Chris smiles, waves enthusiastically and points heavenward mouthing the words "one way." Ed smiles weakly and mocks Chris' "one way" gesture. Chris seems pleased and turns his attention back to Sanders.]*

**Ed:** *[still smiling weakly and sarcastic]* OK, you're a loser... *[turns attention back to Tim who has suddenly become quiet]* Chris and Sanders have been in this deep argument over God since lunch. You know, is there one God or are there lots of them and we just pick one to believe in? I always thought it was just up to us to make the world what we want.

*[Tim becomes increasingly nervous and quiet.]* Nobody can tell me there is really a God that cares about what's going on down here. I mean, it's all just straight out of the big bang and all, right?

**Tim:** *[shrugs and smiles blankly]* Uh well, ummmm, you know, it's complicated and...

**Ed:** It's like—God is just an idea our society creates to explain things, you know?

**Tim:** *[half-hearted, non-committal]* We live in a strange society.

# DEFENDER OR PRETENDER?

**Ed:** I mean, God is just like a crutch made up by people who can't deal with real life, people who can't handle reality.

**Tim:** *[tries to change subject]* Sam Johnson's on crutches.

**Ed:** Chris says we need something bigger than ourselves, so we look to a "God." Like, what's the difference between that and mythology, y'know?

**Tim:** *[weakly]* Ah-huh.

**Ed:** So Tim, what do you think about what Chris says? Hey, I think somebody told me recently that you are a Christian, and I was like, "Not a chance." But...are you?

**Tim:** Uh *[coughs]* Yeah...

**Ed:** So, you believe...what? That God is sitting up there and we all go to heaven?

**Tim:** Well, its just that...well, my parents say...

**Ed:** Parents! My mom doesn't know what she's doing.

*[Ed laughs. Tim looks miserable. The bell rings. Chris pats Sanders on the shoulder and they both find their seats, as do Ed and Tim. Tim is seated closest to the audience at center stage. Teacher begins to speak. All through the talk by Teacher, Tim grows increasingly anxious and unsettled as conviction falls upon him. Ed simply looks smug.]*

**Teacher:** All right, people! Let's pick up where we left off. We were talking about martyrs in world history. If you remember, a martyr is someone who gives his life for a cause or belief, most commonly for a belief in God. We've talked about some of the famous martyrs. But what about each of you? Can anyone think of a cause you would give your life to? How about sticking up for an idea when everyone else thinks otherwise? That's tough, folks. It takes a lot of character, a lot of guts to stand up and put our lives on the line for our ideals. Who can identify with these people, these martyrs? Anyone? What do you wish you could stand up for?

*[Tim slowly but firmly begins to raise his hand.]*

**Teacher:** Tim?

*[Tim stands. Everyone freezes.]*

# DEFENDER OR PRETENDER?

## DISCUSSION

1. When the skit began, Tim was very vocal in his stand and defense of what? When did he start to quiet down a bit? What was happening? Why was Tim having such a difficult time? What do you think Tim was about to say at skit's end?

2. For what beliefs, ideals or issues have you found it most difficult to take a stand in the past? What is the toughest stand you have ever had to take? Why?

3. Read (or summarize) Daniel 3:1-30. Why were these three young Hebrew men so courageous? How was their courage rewarded by God? What good did their stand accomplish? What can we draw from all of this to apply to our own lives? Read 1 Corinthians 10:31-33; 2 Timothy 2:20-22 and Matthew 5:13-16. How does obeying each of these passages require courage? How will our courage be rewarded? How will others benefit from our courage?

4. Someone has said: "Character is always lost when a high ideal is sacrificed on the altar of conformity and popularity." What does this mean? Put it in your own words.

5. The next time you find it difficult to take a stand when you know you should, what will you remember to think? to do?

6. In what one area of your life do you need to take a bolder stand for God or your beliefs?

# JACOB CAN WAIT

## TOPIC: SEXUAL PURITY

## CHARACTERS
Jacob (guy)
rock (guy)
Laban (guy)
donkey (guy; both Jacob and Laban ride him "horse" style)
Rachel (girl)
sheep (the rest of the group, audience)

## PROPS
Bible-times costumes (at least head coverings) and animal costumes.

## NOTE
This narrated skit is **very** loosely based on Genesis 29. Simply read the following narration and have group members act out what is said. Be sure to pause after saying the words in bold to allow time for the appropriate actor to act out what you said. If necessary, repeat these words if an actor misses an action he is to do or if something strikes the audience as particularly funny and you want to repeat it. Use your sense of comic timing as you read.

*Rock is in the middle of stage area.*

Since he couldn't marry the local Canaanite women because they were bad, bad, bad, Jacob traveled to Paddan Aram. First he **walked**, then he **ran**, then he **skipped**...but then he felt like a sissy, so to show he was a brute he hit the floor and did **20 push-ups, the last four one-handed**. Finally, he **ran** up to a big rock that had been pushed over the top of a well. Somehow he **tripped** over it. Then he **stood** on the rock to see what was all around him. He **turned** to the **north, turned south, turned east** and then **turned west**. Then he **fell off** the rock.

About that time, the fair Rachel came **skipping** up to the well as the sheep **ba-a-a-a-a-d** loudly. Rachel **checked her hair, her teeth, her nose, her breath, straightened her skirt and fluffed her hair**. Then she **fluttered her eyes** at Jacob. To impress Rachel, Jacob did what any man would do. He **flexed his muscles** in several weight-lifter poses, **picked** up the rock and **lifted it above his head** with one hand! He staggered under all that weight, but Rachel was obviously **impressed** and **fluttered her eyes** even more fervently and **uttered a strange giggle**. She drew water for her sheep, who **ba-a-a-a-a-d** loudly, as Jacob again **lifted** the rock. Rachel **pretended not to notice**. When she was finished, Jacob **dropped** the rock back over the well.

Page 60

# JACOB CAN WAIT

Jacob **introduced himself** to Rachel in a totally suave, cool way and gave Rachel a **kiss—a brotherly/sisterly kiss**—on each cheek and then one on the forehead, then again and again. Boy, was he glad to see her! She quickly discovered Jacob was an eligible bachelor and became so excited that she did a **cartwheel, spun around five times** and **ran off** to find her father, leaving her sheep with Jacob. The sheep **ba-a-a-a-a-d** loudly.

Not too long after that, Laban (Rachel's father) came **riding** in on his donkey, which looked a lot like Jacob's donkey. Laban's donkey **loudly brayed** a greeting to Jacob. Laban **hugged** Jacob tightly and gave him a **fancy handshake**. Jacob went to work for Laban, so they both **rode around** on Laban's donkey who **brayed** happily as the sheep, **ba-a-a-a-a-ing** loudly, **followed** them, continuing to **b-a-a-a-a-a** loudly as the donkey continued to **bray** loudly.

Finally, there came a time when Laban asked Jacob what he wanted as payment for his work. Jacob **held up seven fingers** to tell Laban he would work seven years to earn Rachel as his wife, for she was lovely in form and beautiful. So for seven years Jacob worked **brushing down** the cattle, **wax on-wax off, wax on-wax off, shoveling manure** and **touching his toes**; **brushing down** the cattle, **wax on-wax off, wax on-wax off, shoveling manure** and **brushing his teeth**; **brushing down** the cattle, **wax on-wax off, wax on-wax off, shoveling manure** and **standing on his head**. Laban came by **riding** his donkey to watch Jacob work and **circled around** a few times.

Though Jacob worked very hard, the seven years "seemed like only a few days to him" because of his great love for Rachel. So then Jacob and Rachel were married, **kissed a very non-sisterly/brotherly kiss** and **rode off** into the sunset on Laban's donkey as the donkey **brayed** happily and the sheep **ba-a-a-a-a'd** loudly.

# JACOB CAN WAIT

## DISCUSSION

1. What is the longest you have waited or hardest you have worked for something you wanted? What was it? How were you able to wait so long? Why?

2. Why did the seven years Jacob had to wait for Rachel seem "like only a few days to him"? How did his great love for Rachel make it easier rather than more difficult to wait? What would have made it tough for Jacob to wait so long to take Rachel as his bride? Why?

3. Read Genesis 29:20-21 (and clear up any background details that might been left fuzzy by the dramatization.) Although Jacob was anxious to lie with Rachel, he waited until the proper time. How might Rachel's feelings and thoughts about Jacob have been changed if he had sneaked in to lie with her before the seven years was up? How might Jacob's thoughts and feelings toward Rachel have changed if he had?

4. How do each of the following relate to waiting vs. not waiting?: Trust, betrayal, a good conscience, shame, feelings of security, commitment, pride, victory vs. defeat.

5. What one thing can you do to stand as firm in purity as Jacob stood? What one action can you take today to commit to remain sexually pure from now until marriage?

# BENCHED

## TOPIC: ATTITUDE

## CHARACTERS
Rick (has read every motivational book known to the modern world)
Nick (Mr. Negative)
Eric
Rachel
Vinnie (tops Nick in negativity)

## PROPS
Bench, bus stop sign and "cigarettes."

## SCENE 1

*Nick enters and goes directly to the bench. He looks back and forth for the bus, then looks at his watch.*

Nick: *[talking to himself]* Dude, what's with this bus? I gotta go...wait a second, I don't have to go anywhere. Cool! *[sits down on the bench, takes out a "cigarette" and begins to pantomime smoking]* Well, another boring day in the armpit of America. Dude, that would be a great band name, the "Armpits of America" with their new single "Life Stinks." That would be cool.

*[Rick strides in quickly, smiling **hugely** and sits **very** close to Nick.]*

Rick: *[nose to nose with Nick, speaking a little loudly.]* Isn't it a wonderful day? I said to myself, "Self, it's going to be a **marvelous** day tomorrow." *[laughs maniacally]* And you know what? *[throws his arms open]* Golly gee willickers, it **is**!

Nick: *[backing away, mocking positivity]* No kidding, dude? You know, I had the same kind of experience, only it went like this: "Self, tomorrow is going to stink just like today stinks. This day is going to be a toilet." And you know what? *[smiling maniacally]* It is." *[suddenly serious, goes back to smoking]*

Page 63

# BENCHED

Rick: [taken aback] My goodness! I'm sorry, I don't believe I know your name. It would be...

Nick: Nick. It would be Nick.

Rick: [excited] Nick? Why, I have an uncle named Nick. Isn't that a crazy coincidence? I mean, I have an uncle named Nick, and then I just happen to sit next to someone I never met named Nick. [laughs maniacally] Isn't that insane?

Nick: That's what I'm thinking. Look, I don't know your name...

Rick: Rick, it's Rick. You can call me Rick. All my friends call me Rick. I consider you my friend, Nick. Call me Rick.

Nick: Rick.

Rick: Yes, Nick.

Nick: Look...Rick...I get the definite sense that you have some pharmaceutical action happening here. **Heavy**, made-it-at-my-house pharmaceutical action...

Rick: [laughs maniacally] Drugs? Heavens no. No drugs in this body. I eat right, work out every day and spend an hour a day reading positive thinking and motivational books. Nick, I'm high on life!

Nick: OK, no pharmaceuticals for the positivity poster child. Surely your mother dropped you on your head as a small child? locked you in a closet for a week or two? Any of this ring a bell for you?

Rick: [suddenly demeanor darkens] I don't know why you had to bring up my childhood. I was never understood as a child. My parents had unresolved inner child issues, codependency issues, dysfunctional families and...[tries to recover] but I'm living in the now. Look, Nick, I feel your negative energy...

Nick: You think so, Rick? That is so perceptive.

Rick: ...and I think if you refocus your inner consciousness, you'll see that all things work in perfect harmony. You need to look into the mirror of life and say, "Hey, I'm OK just as I am." Come on, let's give it a try. [reaches for Nick's hands]

Nick: [pulls away] Dude, you touch me again and our "cosmos-ees" are going to collide big time. Now you take your inner consciousness and slide down a bit.

# BENCHED

| | |
|---|---|
| Rick: | [*with deepest sincerity*] I respect you, and I love you, man. Your honesty is [*starts to get all choked up, turns away*] beautiful. [*sobs softly*] |
| Nick: | [*softly*] Rick? [*pauses, then is all over him verbally*] So what if your mom and dad neglected you? So what if they dressed you funny? I have strong feelings about you. Suck it up, dude, and get on with your life. |
| Rick: | My parents **loved** me...[*nervously, to himself*] Find a happy place, find a happy place...[*stands up and sucks his thumb*] |
| Nick: | Look at you. You're falling apart. What would Daddy think of you now? |
| Rick: | [*gets defensive*] M-M-My father l-l-oves m-m-me. H-H-He just thinks I c-c-could be b-b-better [*Losing it, he exits.*] I got to go now. I got to go now. I got to go **right** now. Bye-bye. Bye-bye. |
| Nick: | See ya, R-R-Rick. |

## SCENE 2

*Eric and Rachel enter and go directly to the bench, not even noticing Nick. They are lovebirds, totally in their own world. Eric and Nick know one another.*

| | |
|---|---|
| Nick: | [*without enthusiasm*] Yo, Eric, what's up? |
| Eric and Rachel: | [*at the same time*] Her! Him! [*get a big kick out of their humor*] |
| Nick: | Oh look, Barbie! Ken! What have you done with Skipper, you maniacs? |
| Eric: | [*without looking*] Oh, hi, Nick. [*Nick sits back on the bench.*] Nick, you know Rachel, the most beautiful goddess on earth, right? |
| Nick: | Uh, no, man. |
| Rachel: | [*distractedly*] Hello, Mick! |
| Nick: | It's Nick. My name is Nick. |
| Rachel: | [*distractedly*] Whatever! |

# BENCHED

**Eric:** *[puts his arms around Rachel]* So what do you think? Isn't she the most beautiful girl you ever saw? I never knew that anyone could be as beautiful as Rachel. Did you, Nick?

**Nick:** *[pauses to think]* Oh, I don't know. There was Wendy Schumaker—the last girl I heard you refer to as a goddess...

*[Rachel becomes irritated]*

...and then there's Samantha Sallinger who, well, what can I say about Samantha but...

**Eric:** *[in response to Rachel's irritation]* Nick...Nick...no reason to trample down past history. I'm a new man with a beautiful, gorgeous woman beside me, for whom my heart is filled with love.

**Rachel:** *[baby talk]* Oh, Eric, my bubbie.

**Nick:** Actually you two do make a good pair for now, but I don't know. In a few years, after you really get to know each other, you'll start to get on each other's nerves. Eric will start to go bald, and Rachel will start to wrinkle up like an old prune and you'll look back over your sad little life and wonder what might have been.

**Rachel:** *[alarmed, touches her face]* Silly, silly Nick. That will never happen to us.

**Eric:** *[also alarmed, runs hands through his hair]* That's right! We're like...Romeo and Juliet. *[to Rachel]* Aren't we, Schnoogums?

**Rachel:** *[playfully]* No, you're the Schnoogums.

**Eric:** No, you are.

*[For a moment, Eric and Rachel resume cuddling, but Rachel seems preoccupied.]*

**Rachel:** Eric? Like if I gained a few pounds and started getting a few wrinkles, you'd still love me the same wouldn't you.

*[Eric starts to answer, then closes his mouth and says nothing.]*

**Rachel:** You **would** still love me...right, Eric?

# BENCHED

**Nick:** Don't you mean Schnoogums?

**Rachel:** Step off, Tick.

**Nick:** That's Nick. *[He exits.]*

**Eric:** *[stumbling]* Honey, I mean the future is just so far away. You know. I mean, we shouldn't get hung up in...

**Rachel:** Remove your hands, please. I would like to go. I need to be alone. *[leaves quickly]*

**Eric:** *[whining]* Schnoogums-woogums, you know I love you.

# SCENE 3

*Nick walks back and sits down. Vinnie promptly enters and sits on the bench. Vinnie is dressed like Nick and carries himself like him as well.*

**Nick:** What's happenin'?

**Vinnie:** Nothing much.

**Nick:** Weird day, huh?

**Vinnie:** Yeah, I know what you mean. This day stinks, man. This place is an armpit.

**Nick:** Uhh, yeah. *[shifts in his seat and pauses for a moment]* I think I know what you mean...

**Vinnie:** Today is in the toilet. Life stinks, man. I hate this place. The people around here, you know they keep me down. This world's going down the tubes, man.

**Nick:** Well, I dunno; I mean, it's all in how you look at it. I mean...this place isn't so bad.

**Vinnie:** *[impatiently]* Dude, dude, do you have a name?

**Nick:** Yeah, I'm Nick.

# BENCHED

**Vinnie:** Well, **Whick**, I don't know what pharmaceuticals are influencing you, but I'm not big on chit-chat and the whole positivity thing. So, step off and relax, OK?

**Nick:** Dude, you are dark, man. Your attitude is bringing me down. I'm outta here.

**Vinnie:** It's a free country. *[talking to himself]* Dude, what's with this bus? I gotta go...wait a second, I don't have to go anywhere. Cool! *[sits down on the bench, takes out a "cigarette" and begins to pantomime smoking]* Well, another boring day in the armpit of America...Dude, that would be a great band name, the "Armpits of America" with their new single "Roll-On Revolution." That would be cool.

## DISCUSSION

1. Would you like being around Nick? Why? How did Nick's attitude (then Vinnie's) affect others negatively?

2. When have you seen this happen in real life—someone's attitude negatively affecting others? When have you seen someone's positive attitude affect the attitudes of others?

3. Read Ephesians 4:29. What does Paul say our attitudes should be when we talk to others? How does what we say reveal our attitudes?

4. How would you define "unwholesome talk"? How can negativity be considered unwholesome talk? In what ways can our attitudes affect others? Give examples from your own life and experience.

5. What aspects of your talk or attitude do you think God wants you to change? What one thing can you begin doing right now to begin that change?

# THE RETREAT

## TOPIC: HOW TO PROCESS SPIRITUAL MOUNTAINTOPS

### CHARACTERS
Youth Pastor
Jacob
Nathaniel
Sarah
Rachel
Extra to walk the signs across the stage
Extras for crowd in Scene 1

### PROPS
Television and remote, empty CD cases (mock-ups of secular CDs), portable CD player, sofa, chair, table, lamp and two posterboard signs, one reading "Winter Retreat, Final Day," the other reading "One Month Later."

## SCENE 1

*Extra holding the "Winter Retreat, Final Day" sign walks across the stage. The youth group cast is all down front of the stage area, facing the stage. Everyone is going nuts, turning to one another for hugs and saying positive things. They cheer for everything people say; it's like a football game.]*

**Youth Pastor:** *[shouts]* So do you love God?

*[Cast goes nuts, cheering and jumping up and down.]*

So you gonna serve Him with all your might?

*[Cast goes nuts, cheering and jumping up and down.]*

*[makes muscles]* What about your strength?

*[Cast goes nuts, cheering and jumping up and down.]*

# THE RETREAT

**Youth Pastor:** What about your heart?

*[Cast goes nuts, cheering and jumping up and down.]*

**Jacob:** *[jumps up in front of the crowd, holding secular CDs]* You know, my life has totally changed! I feel God like I've never felt Him before, man! I can't even see myself **ever** listening to secular music **ever** again.

**Nathaniel:** *[to Sarah]* From now on I'm listening only to Carman and the Gaither Trio—that's all!

**Sarah:** *[to Nathaniel]* I'm only watching Christian TV. Paul and Jan Crouch. That's it!

**Nathaniel:** I don't think I'll even watch TV at all.

**Jacob:** I won't be needing these anymore. *[Throws CDs down on ground and starts stomping on them and breaking them while everyone else goes nuts cheering. Jacob throws himself into the crowd. Everyone catches him and "floats" him around as all leave the area.]*

## SCENE 2

*Extra holding sign saying "One Month Later" walks across the stage before the audience. Stage is set up as a living room. Cast is lounging on living room furniture, totally casual and laid-back, watching television.*

**Jacob:** I've seen this one a million times.

**Nathaniel:** Want to watch it again?

**Jacob:** Sure. *[begins tearing plastic from a new secular CD]*

**Sarah:** *[in a teasing, sarcastic tone]* So, when did you buy that new **secular** CD?

**Jacob:** *[defensive]* This morning.

**Sarah:** What happened to your old ones?

**Jacob:** Shut up. *[cynically]* Oh, did you want to change the channel and watch the "Praise the Lord" show now?

# THE RETREAT

Rachel: Guys, drop it. It's embarrassing to even think about it.

Nathaniel: What?

Rachel: The retreat, Nathaniel. Try to keep up with the conversation.

Nathaniel: *[distantly]* Oh, yeah. That was pretty cool.

Rachel: Cool? What was so cool about it? We made total fools of ourselves! We made a bunch of stupid promises about stupid stuff, and then we came home and...broke them all. I mean, it just seems like it was all so pointless.

Sarah: You make it sound like what we experienced wasn't real.

Rachel: I mean, well, it was real then, but it's not now. I mean, look around you. It hasn't affected us in the long run.

Nathaniel: *[matter-of-factly]* It's affected me...It affects me every year. It's always that way. You know how it goes at camps and retreats. You go, you get pumped up, on fire, turned on...all those catchy youth leader slogans...and then you come home and...uh...reality hits.

Sarah: Yeah, but what is reality?

Rachel: *[sarcastically]* Oooohhh.

Nathaniel: It's this. This is reality. Us in this room. Do you see anybody to witness to? *[looks under seat cushion]* Oh, hello, do you need Jesus? Anyone here need help in fulfilling their spiritual needs? See?

Jacob: I think you're going too far, Nate.

Nathaniel: Well, its' true!

Jacob: I know you're not trying to tear down anybody's faith.

Nathaniel: I'm just saying, we can't keep it up forever...I don't think it's possible.

Rachel: Oh, you think so? Why do you say that?

Nathaniel: You know, all the promises we made about not listening to music or watching TV.

Page 71

# THE RETREAT

**Sarah:** Yeah, why did we react that way?

**Nathaniel:** Well, during those days at camp, was God up in heaven going, "Well, ya' know, I'm glad that they are all experiencing My love and everything, but what I really want is for Nate to quit watching the Simpsons."?

**Jacob:** What is the bottom line of our experience?

**Rachel:** Pastor Todd says the bottom line is...

**Everyone:** *[shouting]* Commitment!

**Jacob:** Yeah, but what I'm asking is, was what we experienced at the retreat really God or not?

**Sarah:** Yeah, was it real or, like my dad says, just teenage emotionalism?

**Rachel:** It was emotion.

**Nathaniel:** No, it was God.

**Jacob:** Emotionalism vs. God. Next on Geraldo.

**Sarah:** Well, I mean, maybe that is what life is all about. Ups and downs. I mean, we were allowing the Holy Spirit total control of our lives. We were reading our Bibles and praying and getting along. It was good. I liked it. Now some of the people who were closest to me won't even talk to me.

**Rachel:** Yeah, whatever.

**Sarah:** I wish we could just live at camp.

**Nathaniel:** We can't live there, but we can go back.

**Sarah:** Maybe if we keep going back every year, we'll learn a little more and a little more, and then we can bring camp home with us. And it will last a little longer and a little longer until one day we wake up and realize... hey, it's the day that we go to camp, and I'm still as close to God as I was last year...Ohhh, I'm sorry. I was rambling.

**Rachel:** *[hugs Sarah]* Ohhh Sarah, you are so sweet. I wish I had your heart.

# THE RETREAT

Jacob: And I wish I had your hair.

Nathaniel: I wish I had your...money.

## DISCUSSION

1. What was the most exciting, thrilling time you ever had in your life? Do you feel the same way right now as you did when you were in the middle of that experience? Why not? Does that make your thrilling experience any less genuine or valuable? Why? What would be the problem with expecting to constantly experience times like this?

2. From what you heard from each of these youth group members, how would you describe their hearts? What evidence do you have that they desire a more intense experience with God? Why? What may be keeping them from experiencing more "fire" in their spiritual lives?

3. Read John 15:1-16. How do we remain in Christ (stay close to Him)? What is the evidence that we are doing so? What benefits do we realize from doing so?

4. Someone has said our goal as Christians should not be about "swinging from vine to vine but about clinging to the vine." What does this mean? How does this apply to spiritual mountaintop experiences?

5. Obviously spiritual mountaintops aren't bad, and it is condescending to say they are merely teenage emotionalism. What purpose do such experiences serve in our spiritual lives? What can we take from these experiences that can help us abide in the vine (more closely walk with God)? What is the best ongoing benefit you have received from a spiritual mountaintop experience?

6. In what do you desire to draw closer to God (more closely walk with God)? Why?

*(Close by praying for each person to be drawn closer to God.)*

# MY GIRLFRIEND'S BACK AND THERE'S GONNA BE TROUBLE

## TOPICS: DATING, PARENTS, JUDGMENT

### CHARACTERS
Ma and Pa (very conservative, older couple)
Kevin (average Christian teenage guy)
Ezadora ("alternative" girl who wears all black clothing, white lipstick outlined in black and clip-on earrings on her nose, lip, forehead and cheeks so as to appear fully pierced)

### PROPS
Glasses of lemonade, two rocking chairs, cassette recording of big band (or country music), cassette recording of alternative "complaint rock" and cassette player.

*Ma and Pa are sitting on their porch enjoying a beautiful, sunny day. Play big band music in the background.*

**Ma:** Leonard, you've done it again! The lawn is immaculate! Romance really builds in my heart when you weed-whack that way.

**Pa:** Really?

**Ma:** Oh, yes. In fact, I am feeling romantic right now just staring at the way you have edged the sidewalk. Hold my hand!

**Pa:** It looks like I will be using the weed-whacker more.

[Ma and Pa sip lemonade.]

**Ma:** The birds, the bees, the flowers...Leonard, what a beautiful afternoon.

**Pa:** Kevin is bringing his newest girlfriend by this afternoon.

**Ma:** Really? It's so cute to see him start to date such pretty little girls.

**Pa:** Just as long as they are serving God, I don't care what they look like.

**Ma:** I wonder who it will be today. I thought he had already dated every girl in his class.

# MY GIRLFRIEND'S BACK AND THERE'S GONNA BE TROUBLE

Pa: She's new, I guess. Moved in from Los Angeles.

Ma: Such nice people in California.

Pa: Yeah, nice people.

*[Kevin enters alone. Ma goes to greet him.]*

Ma: Kevin, darling, you're home. How was school?

Kevin: Ah, great. Really.

Pa: Where is your new little friend?

Kevin: Uh, she's coming. I *[pause]* don't know if she is exactly what you have in mind for me. I want you both to promise me you will have an open mind.

Ma: We love everyone, honey. We're Christians.

Pa: That's right.

Kevin: Ezadora, it's OK. You can come out now.

Ma: Eza-what-a?

*[Play alternative "complaint rock" as Ezadora enters. Ma faints.]*

Kevin: Ma, you OK?

Pa: Here, she needs something to smell to bring her back. I don't have any smelling salts. Kevin, give me your shoe.

*[Kevin gives him his shoe. Ma revives and stands back up.]*

Ma: Uh, oh, I'm so sorry. I don't know what came over me!

Pa: So, it's nice to meet you.

Ma: What might your name be?

Ezadora: It is Ezadora, but it might be Ezzy.

Ma: Excuse me?

# MY GIRLFRIEND'S BACK AND THERE'S GONNA BE TROUBLE

**Ezadora:** I said, "Ezadora." They call me Ezzy.

**Pa:** Essay?

**Kevin:** No, Dad. EZZZy.

**Pa:** Oh, yeah. Pleased to meet you Essay, uh Ezzy. *[Pa extends hand for a handshake. Ma seems afraid and awkwardly avoids shaking Ezadora's hand.]* I'm Leonard, and this is my wife, Mabel. We're Kevin's parents. We've heard a lot about you...

**Ma:** *[cuts him off]* But apparently not near enough. So, Ezzy, tell us a little bit about yourself.

**Ezadora:** Well, I'm like, you know, an original! I believe totally in like individualism and freedom and in rescuing the spotted screech eagle. And, well, I'm the voice for a band that does songs on those three issues. That's like all there is...ya know...that's me!

**Pa:** Well...that's nice.

**Kevin:** Isn't she amazing?

**Ma:** Oh, that and more. That is, I'd like to hear more—about your parents, California, your intentions for my son, etc. *[Stares incredulously at Ezadora with an "I-can't-believe-this-is-happening-to-me-what-will-others-think?" look]*

**Kevin:** Mother, stop staring.

**Ezadora:** Dad abandoned my mom and me when I was 2, and we've scraped along to survive since then. Like two months ago she got this job out here, and here we are. We floated in just over a month ago. So far, so good. As far as men, well Mom and I have had our problems. The guy she's living with now is pretty cool, though.

**Kevin:** Mother...

**Ezadora:** Oh, you know, the most incredible thing happened last month...

**Pa:** *[stage whispers]* Ma, **stop** staring!

**Ma:** I couldn't help but notice your **many** earrings.

# MY GIRLFRIEND'S BACK AND THERE'S GONNA BE TROUBLE

Kevin: Here we go.

Ma: Does it hurt to have your nose, lip, forehead and cheeks pierced?

Ezadora: Well, like, it hurt at first, but now I don't even think much about it. I'm just expressing my individuality, protesting the feminine stereotypes imposed on us sisters since the beginning of time in our male-dominated world. You know what I mean, Mabel?

Ma: *[in sing-song fashion]* Kevin, might I have a word with you...alone?

Kevin: What? Oh sure, Ma.

*[Ma and Kevin walk off to the right as Ezzy and Pa pantomime pointing toward various areas of the yard and discussing them. During their entire conversation Ma and Kevin turn occasionally to smile toward Ezadora and Pa, while hissing their lines to one another.]*

Ma: Is this a joke—darling?

Kevin: What do you mean?

Ma: I mean, what is going on in that head of yours—honey?

Kevin: Ma, don't judge a movie by its preview.

Ma: Kevin, I would never judge anyone, but this movie is rated "R." You hear me? R—as in run the other way. I don't have to be Siskel and Ebert to know that—sweetheart.

Kevin: I knew you would judge her before you got to know her.

Ma: I am sorry if you are offended that I am trying to be a parent here—darling.

Kevin: It's fine to be a parent, but you haven't even given Ezadora a chance.

Ma: OK, you want one more chance. Here it is. Is she a Christian?

Pa: *[cuts Ma off]* Honey, Ezzy was just telling me about becoming a Christian last month. It's a great testimony. Come hear it!

Kevin: *[gives Ma the look]* You were saying?

# MY GIRLFRIEND'S BACK AND THERE'S GONNA BE TROUBLE

Ma: [*trying to recover*] That is, I mean rated R for Redeemed.

[*Everyone freezes.*]

## DISCUSSION

1. In your objective opinion, were Kevin's parents within their rights to be concerned about him dating Ezadora? Why?

2. Should Kevin be able just to choose whom he wants to date with no interference from his parents? Why?

3. What could he have done to help his parents prepare for what he knew was coming? Should he have felt more responsibility to do that? Why?

4. Are feelings of affection and attraction the only reliable criteria for deciding whom to date? What are some other criteria that should be considered? Why? What do you think of the following criteria: the person must be a Christian? the person must share or exceed my standards of morality? the person should have a maturing relationship with God? the person should be someone of whom my parents approve?

5. How do each of the following verses apply to dating: 1 Corinthians 6:14-17, 18-20, 15:33; Ephesians 6:2-3 and Philippians 4:6-7? *(List these on a chalkboard for everyone to see.)* What else do you feel Scripture has to say about girlfriend/boyfriend relationships? In light of these Scripture passages, why is dating people based primarily on the criteria of affection and physical attraction dangerous? Illustrate this from what you have observed in the dating relationships of others.

6. Describe the person you would consider to be the dream date. What physical qualities and personality characteristics would they possess? Describe his or her spiritual life.

7. In light of all we have discussed concerning dating, what one change do you feel you should make in your dating?

# MALL TRIP

## TOPICS: GOD'S FAVOR, PRAYER

### CHARACTERS
Jesse (a guy)
Mark (whiny type)
Wanda
Five extras for sound effects.

### PROPS
Three chairs (to be used as a car), play money and set of car keys.

*Stage has two chairs facing audience, with one chair behind them but visible to audience. Jesse is the driver, Wanda sits next to him, and Mark is in the back seat. Extras periodically make the sounds of numerous cars and beeping horns in the background.*

Mark: [*annoyed*] This traffic is a real pain. Ever since that new mall opened, there are cars everywhere. You can't go anywhere without a traffic jam. I hate that mall, Jesse. I hate that mall.

Wanda: Jesse, we are still going, aren't we? I mean, I thought we were going.

Mark: What?

Jesse: Wanda wants to go to the mall.

Mark: [*throws his hands up in frustration*] Is anyone listening to me? Does anyone hear me when I talk?

Jesse: [*jokingly*] I'm sorry, Mark, did you say something? I wasn't listening. [*Jesse and Wanda laugh.*]

Mark: Go ahead. Get your laughs. Oh man, look! We're stuck in traffic. We're dead. Nobody is moving. [*becoming more frustrated*] Beep the horn, Jesse. Get that guy moving ahead of us.

Wanda: Jesse, I don't think that's such a good idea.

# MALL TRIP

**Mark:** *[annoyed]* Will you blow the horn?

**Jesse:** I've got to agree with Wanda. I really don't think it's a good idea.

**Mark:** This is nuts. I'll do it. *[As he is reaches to blow the horn, Jesse and Wanda try to stop him, but it's too late. He blows the horn. Extra makes loud horn sound.]*

**Wanda:** Real mature, Mark. Now he's looking at us.

**Mark:** *[leans out the window]* Hey, what's your problem, moron? Drive it or park it! *[sits back in the car]* Can you believe the nerve of that guy? Who does he think he is?

**Jesse:** Pastor Kevin's dad.

**Mark:** That guy shouldn't even—what's that?

**Wanda:** He said that the guy you just honked at is Pastor Kevin's dad. You know, our youth pastor? The same pastor who illustrates the power of God by denting soda cans with his forehead?

**Mark:** *[panicking]* Oh, man. He's always asking for volunteers for that stuff. *[leans out the window]* Sorry, Mr. Harris! I love you, man. *[more desperately]* Ah, ah honk if you love Jesus. *[sits back]* Do you think he bought that?

**Jesse and Wanda:** *[pause, then together]* No!

**Wanda:** Jesse, why don't we pray that the traffic will start to move?

**Jesse:** That's a good idea.

**Mark:** Oh yeah, right! You're going to say a prayer, and the traffic is going to start moving? You're good, Jesse, but not that good.

**Jesse:** Dear Lord...*[pause]*

**Wanda:** Jesse, Mark—look! The traffic is moving. *[Extras sing out "Hallelujah!" once and stop.]*

**Mark:** *[Mark looks around.]* Oh, man, I don't believe this. You only said two words. I could pray for hours. It's got to be a coincidence. It's got to be.

# MALL TRIP

**Wanda:** There doesn't seem to be any place to park. You're right, Mark; it really is crowded.

**Jesse:** Let me see if I can get us a spot closer to the entrance. This way we don't have too far walk.

**Mark:** What, are you crazy? Those are the spots that get taken first. You could wait for an hour and still not get a space. *[pause]* I have an idea! *[sarcastically]* Jesse, why don't you pray for a spot right at the front door? God seems to listen to everything you say.

**Jesse:** Dear Lord...*[pause, then extras sing "Hallelujah!"]*

**Wanda:** Jesse! *[points to a spot that is open]*

**Mark:** *[puts his hands over his face]* I don't believe this.

**Jesse:** *[surprised]* Wow! *[excitedly]* Hey, Mark, look—a spot right up front. Cool!

*[Jesse pulls the car into the spot. Extras make the sound of the car braking and the ignition turning off with a backfire. All three in car should shake together as the car turns off and quits, then backfires They all get out of the car.]*

**Jesse:** Wait a minute. Let me set the alarm. *[He points his keys and exaggeratedly presses a button. Extra makes a "beep" sound].* OK, let's go. *[They take a few steps.]* Oh, no! *[looks into his wallet]* I forgot to bring money.

**Wanda:** Why don't you pray—

**Mark:** *[puts his hands over his ears]* Oh man, I don't want to hear this.

**Jesse:** Dear Lord...*[Extras sing "Hallelujah!"]*

**Mark:** Why me, Lord? Why me?

**Wanda:** Jesse, what's under your shoe?

**Jesse:** *[surprised]* Gee, Wanda, let's take a look. *[lifts his shoe]* I don't believe it. It's a 100 dollar bill.

**Mark:** Oh, for crying out loud. **This** is too much. *[turns away in disgust]*

**Jesse:** Wait, Mark! Don't move. It looks like you have something under your shoe.

# MALL TRIP

**Mark:** You're kidding, right? *[gets excited]* Stuff like this never happens to me. *[lifts his foot and examines it, then looks away in disgust]* But stuff like this does. Can't people walk their dogs someplace else? *[pause]* Jesse, what's the deal? You and I grew up together. We both go to the same church. Why are you getting blessed so much? *[wipes his shoe on the ground]*

**Jesse:** Mark, I don't know, but let's go inside and get something to eat. We can talk more about it.

**Mark:** Yeah, I guess. By the way, I know who's buying! *[Extras sing "Hallelujah!"]*

## DISCUSSION

1. With whom do you most identify, Mark or Jesse? Why (or in what way)?

2. Why was Mark so annoyed at the favor that Jesse had?

3. What was realistic about this skit? unrealistic? How was this skit accurate concerning what brings God's favor to our lives? inaccurate?

4. Read Proverbs 3:1-6 (emphasizing verses 3-4) and 12:2. What are some keys for gaining the favor of God? What qualities in us does the Lord bless? Why do you think He blesses these qualities? How is God's favor defined in these Scripture passages? How would you define the Lord's favor?

5. Have you ever had a day like Jesse had? Tell us what happened. When have you sensed that you had the Lord's favor and special blessing?

6. In what way do you most need to experience God's favor and receive a blessing from Him today? Ask Him for it now.

# HEART BEACH

## TOPICS: RIGHTEOUSNESS, HOLINESS

### CHARACTERS
Tony

Annette

Lust and Anger (guys or girls, each wearing black, an appropriate sign and green crepe paper as seaweed)

One person to hold up signs

### PROPS
Beach towels, two lounge chairs, two rakes, garbage bags, boom box, green crepe paper, two signs on yarn necklaces ("LUST" and "ANGER"), cassette (or CD) of beach music and four crowd instruction signs: "Ocean and Surf" (shhhh), "Seagulls" (kaw-kaw), "Hiss!" (ssssss) and "Football Cheer" (shake fists while yelling OOH,OOH,OOH).

*Lounge chairs, boom box and beach towels are at center stage. Music is playing softly from boom box. Just before the skit begins, have the audience practice the sound effects as you hold up each sign. Be sure Lust and Anger characters stay out of sight until they are to enter. After a brief sound effect rehearsal with the audience, begin the skit. Hold up signs as scripted and randomly as you choose. It can also add comic effect to occasionally hold up the wrong sign.*

*Hold up Ocean and Surf sign, raising it and lowering it to create rises and falls. Hold up Seagulls sign. After about 15 seconds, soften the surf sounds by lowering it. Tony and Annette enter and busily begin raking up imaginary trash from the beach and putting it into their bags.*

**Tony:** *[raking]* Good grief! I can't believe how much trash washed up on shore last night. We cleaned this very same part of the beach yesterday!

**Annette:** *[puts down rake and sits in lounge chair]* Well, it looks pretty good now. Let's cool down and enjoy the last day we have here at summer camp. I am gonna miss this place.

*[Hold up Seagulls sign.]*

# HEART BEACH

**Annette:** However, I **won't** miss these annoying seagulls. This has been a great camp. I wish I could feel God's presence back home like I do here.

**Tony:** *[tosses down rake and sits in lounge chair]* Ya know, I was thinking the same thing! I always feel so...I don't know...so clean here.

**Annette:** Clean, refreshed and renewed, I know what you mean. Our hearts are clean, our minds are clean, our socks are clean and our beach is clean. Yup, all clean.

*[Hold up Hiss sign. Lust crawls from the back of the room toward Tony and Annette as both of them ad-lib conversation about camp. Both are reclining and relaxing with eyes closed. Hold up "Hiss" sign intermittently when it seems appropriate. Lust hams it up with wild, enticing gestures all around Tony and Annette, who are both unaware of it. Tony opens his eyes and looks at Annette in a "new light." Lust curls up around his chair.]*

**Tony:** *[undergoes a shift in personality to be more aggressive—but still Tony]* Annette, I've been meaning to tell you just how fine you are...

*[Hold up Football Cheer sign.]*

**Annette:** Excuse me?

*[Hold up Hiss sign.]*

**Tony:** I mean, just how **faithful** you are...

**Annette:** *[suspiciously]* Uh-huuuuh.

**Tony:** ...and that I've enjoyed looking at you...

*[Hold up Football Cheer sign.]*

**Annette:** Uh-HUH!

*[Hold up Hiss sign.]*

**Tony:** I mean, **learning** with you here in our little work detail on the beach every day.

**Annette:** Oh, I think I understand...

# HEART BEACH

**Tony:** *[Tony reaches over and places his hand on Annette's hand.]* I hope we can get closer when we get back...

*[Hold up Football Cheer sign.]*

**Annette:** *[smiles]* Let go of the hand. *[Tony pulls his hand back. Hold up "Hiss" sign.]*

**Tony:** That is, **closer to God.**

**Annette:** *[seems interested]* Is that so?

*[Hold up Hiss sign. Anger stomps in, making its way to Annette. Hold up Hiss sign as desired. Anger crawls next to Annette's chair and curls up around it.]*

**Annette:** *[loud, with bravado]* Looking for a little end-of-the-retreat romantic rendezvous are we, Antonio old boy?

**Tony:** *[doesn't quite catch the change in Annette]* Of course...not.

**Annette:** Sally ditched you two days ago because she felt you two should be friends, and you can't deal with the date deficit can you?

**Tony:** No. Wait! That's not true. Its just that I've really enjoyed your companionship—**company**. You've been a real sister to me this week.

**Annette:** Oh, right—**sister! Sorority sister** in your mind! Don't give me that. All guys are the same. Nice for a while, play the good Christian guy routine, then look out, sister—double agent! I know what's really on your foul, seething, lust-consumed mind!

*[Hold up Hiss sign.]*

**Tony:** You do? Uh, I mean, you think you do. Well, no you don't.

**Annette:** You were supposed to be studying God's Word at this camp, but I bet you've studied more human anatomy than anything!

**Tony:** If that were the case, I sure wouldn't be looking this way.

*[Annette gasps. Hold up Hiss sign.]*

I mean... *[as if waking up]* Hey, wait a second. Annette, I am so sorry. I don't know what got into me. What's going on?

# HEART BEACH

**Annette:** We both lost it for a minute. I'm sorry, too. Whew! I'm confused. I thought we were going to have a great day here on the beach—our very last day of camp.

**Tony:** I feel so bad. I don't even feel clean anymore.

*[Annette moves her leg off the chair to the ground and steps on Anger.]*

**Annette:** Oh, no! Where did this trash come from?

*[Suddenly both are aware of Lust and Anger.]*

**Tony:** Hey, it washed up around me, too. What's the deal? Where did this stuff come from? We just cleaned our beach! Annette, get the rakes—and quick!

*[Tony and Annette chase Lust and Anger from the stage. Hold up Football Cheer sign, then Ocean and Surf sign and finally the Seagulls sign.]*

# HEART BEACH

## DISCUSSION

1. What did the beach represent for Tony and Annette? In regard to righteousness and holiness, what was the message of this skit?

2. Read Ephesians 4:17-24. How can you "be made new in the attitude of your minds"? Why is what you think so important? What might the final outcome of dwelling on impure thoughts be?

3. Read Ephesians 4:25–5:10. According to this passage, what are some ways we are to think and act? What are some things we are not to do? Why?

   *(Have group members form pairs or trios and discuss the following questions.)*

4. This passage identifies enemies of righteousness: lust, anger, doubt, stealing, impure language, greed, malice and more. Which of these (or others) do you most need to have cleaned away from the "beach" of your heart? Why?

5. What one thing will you do to keep your beach clean from this?

   *(Have pairs or trios pray for one another according to what is shared.)*

# TESTED AND TRIUMPHANT

## TOPICS: TRUST IN GOD, VICTORY

### CHARACTERS
Jack (loves God, but is distracted by personal things and doubt)
Michael (the Angel)
Denzel (the Demon)
Extras (members of Jack's church)

### PROPS
Any furniture that suggests a church setting (pulpit, chairs in rows, etc.).

*Jack is standing with others from his church. Those around him should pantomime activities common in a worship service throughout this skit (kneeling and praying, lifting hands in praise, etc.). Suddenly Denzel slinks in and positions himself about 10 feet behind Jack.*

**Jack:** *[praying aloud, but those around him cannot hear]* Lord, it's been a tough week. I got accepted at State College, but there isn't any money. Dad's been out of work, and Mom is only working part time. They fight a lot, and to top all that off, the last place I want to be right now is here at church.

**Denzel:** All right! That's what I like to hear. This one's gonna be eeeasssssy. *[to Jack]* Yo, Jack, you've prayed about all these things before. God must not be listening—if He's even there at all.

**Jack:** You know, God, I wonder if You're even hearing my prayers. Hello? Are You even there?

*[Denzel takes a step closer to Jack. Each time Jack gives in to doubt, Denzel draws closer to Jack. Michael enters the stage about 10 feet behind Jack, just off to the right. When Jack listens to Michael, Michael moves closer to him and Denzel moves farther away. Denzel notices Michael.]*

**Denzel:** *[annoyed]* Hey, what are you doing here? What is it with you, Michael? Every time I'm going to have some fun, you ruin it. Why don't you go row a boat ashore or something?

# TESTED AND TRIUMPHANT

**Michael:** *[very cool]* Denzel, God has some big plans for Jack, so don't get in my way. Watch and weep, baby. *[to Jack]* You know that God loves you and is with you now.

**Jack:** Lord, I don't know what I was thinking. I know You're here with me. *[Michael moves closer as Denzel steps away.]*

**Denzel:** Of course God's there; everyone seems to know that except these humans who have to see it to believe it. Perception is reality. *[to Jack]* But He feels so far away, doesn't He?

**Jack:** But You seem so far away. Why? *[Denzel proudly takes another step forward.]*

**Denzel:** *[to Michael]* Wow! Looks like the bonus round. *[sarcastically]* Michael, you still here? You're bein' **awfully** quiet. *[laughs]*

**Michael:** *[to Jack]* Keep trying, Jack. Push through, man. Concentrate on God. Remember the Scripture Pastor Tate quoted just a minute ago, "Don't be surprised at the sufferings." Don't be! Don't be surprised. Be strong! Trust God!

**Jack:** *[gathers strength]* I shouldn't be surprised at this stuff, just like Pastor Tate said. I will get through this. I trust You, God. *[He raises his hands and begins to praise God silently. Michael takes a big step forward.]*

**Denzel:** *[to Michael]* Touche'! So you want to play tough. Here we go. *[to Jack]* Hey, Jack, this is all well and good, but you know what reality is. This service is a little more than an hour long. Then you have to go home. Dad's been drinking. You'll lie awake, tossing and turning, your stomach in knots while he rants and raves at your mom—again.

*[Not waiting for a response, Denzel struts forward in a big step. Jack's hands begin to fall.]*

**Jack:** *[angry]* Why does he have to yell at her like that? Where are You when that happens? Where are You? If You are totally real, where are You when that stuff happens? What is happening to me? I feel so confused.

**Michael:** *[to Jack]* Jack, why are you thinking these thoughts? If everything seems confusing, then you know it isn't from God. Think, Jack. Where are these thoughts coming from?

**Denzel:** *[to Michael]* That's a low blow. Are you sure you're not one of us?

# TESTED AND TRIUMPHANT

**Jack:** What am I thinking? I know my dad loves my mom, but he needs help. He needs prayer. *[He begins to pray. Michael comes one regular step and one giant step toward Jack.]*

**Denzel:** *[protesting Michael's extra steps]* Hey, wait a minute. You can't take all these steps. It's not fair.

**Michael:** Oh, it's fair. One for the thought change and a big one for praying.

**Denzel:** Thought change! Hmmm...now here's a thought change. *[to Jack]* Hey, Jack, how's your girlfriend Linda doing? Oh, my mistake—**ex**-girlfriend. She dumped you, didn't she? *[Jack covers his face with his hands. Denzel takes a step forward.]*

**Michael:** Now **that's** low!

**Denzel:** *[to Michael]* Dude, I wrote the book.

**Michael:** *[pointing up]* But **He** wrote **The Book**. Excuse me. I'm going to need some walking room. *[to Jack]* Jack, don't you remember what God showed you about His plan for you in that break-up?

**Jack:** *[uncovers his face]* God, I know Linda and I had to break-up; that relationship was pulling me away from You. It was a blessing. Your plans are only good for me. *[Michael takes a step forward.]*

**Michael:** Thank Him, Jack.

**Jack:** Thanks, God. *[Michael takes another step. From this point on, Michael does all the moving until he is directly next to Jack and Denzel is still in the back. Even when Denzel tries to tempt him, Jack can't hear him.]*

**Denzel:** *[to Jack, sarcastically]* Why don't you thank Him for the time you got caught trying to sneak out of school.?

**Jack:** Lord, I even thank You for the time I got caught sneaking out of school. You taught me to watch who I hang around with. Thanks! Man, I haven't thought of that in years. That's weird.

**Denzel:** *[puzzled]* Hey, It's not supposed to work like that. *[to Jack]* Hey Jack, what about your hair today—pretty bad, huh? Remember how Denise ignored you in the hall? What about the guys? They made big Saturday plans, and you weren't invited!

# TESTED AND TRIUMPHANT

**Michael:** *[to Jack]* Jack, remember to give thanks to God in all things.

**Jack:** Lord, my life is so crazy right now, but somehow I know it will all work out. I'll tell You the truth—I don't know how You're going to do it; I just know You will. *[Michael keeps coming closer.]*

**Denzel:** *[whining to Michael]* Hey, not so close. He can't hear me.

**Jack:** Man, this is great. *[praising God]* There is none like You, God—none.

**Michael:** *[to Jack]* You feel His presence, don't you, Jack? He's here. He's in your words.

**Denzel:** *[frightened and screams]* Aaaahhhhhh! I'm outta here!

**Michael:** *[doesn't notice Denzel's departure]* Keep praising Him, Jack. He is here, and He loves you.

**Jack:** I love You, Lord. I'm sorry for how I've been. It's been so hard, but You **are** always with me.

**Michael:** And He'll never leave you. He cares too much for you.

**Jack:** Thanks for being there for me. *[Jack is now in full praise and worship. Both Michael and Jack freeze.]*

# TESTED AND TRIUMPHANT

## DISCUSSION

1. Why did Jack keep going up and down in his trust of God? How was Jack's anxiety hindering his peace and undermining his trust in God? What finally happened that cemented his ability to trust God in this circumstance?

2. When Jack listened to Michael, not only was Michael able to draw closer but Denzel was driven farther away. When Jack listened to Denzel, though Denzel drew closer, Michael never moved away. What is the significance of this?

3. Tell us of a situation or a relationship in which you found it difficult to trust God. How did you handle it?

4. Read Psalm 22:7-8. Have you ever felt like your trust in God was being mocked by others? What happened? Have you ever felt mocked "on the inside" as Jack did in this skit? What did you do?

5. Read verse 24. Is God listening to you when you cry out to Him? How does knowing this help you?

6. What can you decide today to do the next time your trust in God is mocked "on the inside"? when it's mocked by others? Knowing what you know now, how would you handle the situation you shared in question 3?

7. In what one situation or relationship are you right now finding it most difficult to trust God? What one thing will you keep in mind to grow strong in your trust of God in this matter?

# DARRELL AND LARRY DISCUSS JOBS

## TOPICS: DILIGENCE, SELF-MOTIVATION

## Characters
Darrell
Larry (if possible, someone who can play the guitar)
Extra

## Note
Both characters should be clothed in denim, rock band T-shirts and wearing long-haired wigs.

## Props
Guitar, television on table, sofa (or two lounge chairs), cassette recording of a cool guitar riff and cassette player.

*Darrell and Larry sit very casually on sofa. They look extremely apathetic and speak with a "hey dude" tone of voice with all the pauses and body language that go with it.*

| | |
|---|---|
| Darrell: | Is there anything good on TV? |
| Larry: | Probably. |
| Darrell: | You got the remote? |
| Larry: | [thinks a moment] Naw, man. Isn't it sittin' over there by you? [Darrell turns slowly and looks next to him, then back.] |
| Darrell: | I don't see it, man. |
| Larry: | Well, look around for it. [long pause] |
| Darrell: | Ah, that's OK. We don't have to watch TV. |
| Larry: | That remote's probably sittin' around here somewhere. |
| Darrell: | Then why don't you look for it, man? [pause] |
| Larry: | I see your point. |

# DARRELL AND LARRY DISCUSS JOBS

**Darrell:** Hey, you know...this one time I was watchin' TV, and there were, like, these guys who ski for a living.

**Larry:** They do what?

**Darrell:** They ski, and people, like, pay to watch them or something.

**Larry:** Are you serious? [*pause*]

**Darrell:** No, no, no, no, no...I know what it was. They ski, and people pay to have them teach them how to ski. That's what it was.

**Larry:** People pay these guys money, and that's all they do is teach people how to ski?

**Darrell:** Yeah, and they go on rescues and stuff like that.

**Larry:** It was on TV, man. It's not real.

**Darrell:** No, it wasn't, like, a show. I mean, it was a show, but not, like, with a story or nothin'. It was just, like, information.

**Larry:** [*slowly*] An **information** show.

**Darrell:** Yeah. You know, 'cause there's, like, two kinds of shows. There's shows that have, like, a story, and there's shows that teach you stuff.

**Larry:** I never really thought about it that way.

**Darrell:** Yeah. Like, the news.

**Larry:** Yeah?

**Darrell:** The news, like, teaches you stuff. Like, about the world.

**Larry:** But that's kind of like a story.

**Darrell:** What? How is the news like a story?

**Larry:** Well, you know. They have, like, news stories.

**Darrell:** But that's not a story. You never see Dan Rather at home talking to his wife, and, like, solving his personal problems.

# DARRELL AND LARRY DISCUSS JOBS

**Larry:** So?

**Darrell:** So if you did, it would be a story. [pause]

**Larry:** That's an interesting point.

**Darrell:** Hey man, what are we gonna do after we graduate?

**Larry:** What? You mean, like, for a job?

**Darrell:** Yeah.

**Larry:** I don't know. Why?

**Darrell:** I don't know. I was just thinking about it. I had, like, this idea. Maybe we could open an electronics store or something.

**Larry:** Yeah?

**Darrell:** Yeah. You know, a store that sells all kinds of appliances and stuff. And then we could, like, get real rich. And buy stocks and bonds and stuff.

**Larry:** I like James Bond, but I think I'd rather spend my money on a cool car.

**Darrell:** Yeah. So what do you say? Are we gonna do it?

**Larry:** Wait. Don't you have to, like, have good math skills to do something like that?

**Darrell:** Oh...yeah...math skills.

**Larry:** Are you sure that remote control isn't sittin' over there by you?

**Darrell:** I'm not sure.

[*Larry slowly picks up a guitar that sits next to his chair. He suddenly plays a really fast, complex riff on it. (Or play a prerecorded fast, complex electric guitar riff as he pantomimes it.) When he is done, he sets the guitar down by his side. Pause.*]

**Darrell:** You're pretty good at that, man.

**Larry:** Thanks, bro.

# DARRELL AND LARRY DISCUSS JOBS

Darrell:   You ought to, like, play in a band, man.

Larry:   Don't you have to, like, practice and stuff?

Darrell:   Oh...yeah.

## DISCUSSION

1. In what way are Larry and Darrell "challenged"? What seem to be their weaknesses? What is missing in their lives? What are some words you could use to describe Darrell and Larry?

2. On their present course, what do you think will happen in the lives of these two guys in the next year? the next five years? Why?

3. Read Proverbs 6:6-11. What are some characteristics of ants that we are supposed to emulate? What will befall the sluggard? Besides monetary poverty, what other kinds of poverty might we experience if we are lazy?

4. Would you describe yourself as a self-starting, self-motivated, hard-working person or a sluggard (slacker)? Why?

5. In what one way do you lack motivation or have you found it difficult to put forth your best effort? What "poverty" might you experience if you don't get motivated and work harder in this area? For example, studying chemistry: The poverty I will suffer if I don't study harder for this will be a bad grade and a suffering grade point average. What one thing will you do today to work harder and be more self-motivated in this area?